The Leadership Arena

Mastering the Art of Leadership through *SHIP-building*™, and Other Secrets to Individual and Organizational Success!

Richard Spector

Table of Contents

Acknowledgements 4
Foreword 6
Introduction 8
Chapter One: What is SHIP-Building™? 20
Chapter Two: What Leadership is NOT. 25
Chapter Three: MENTORSHIP – Laying the Keel 37
Chapter Four: STUDENTSHIP 52
Chapter Five: DIRECTORSHIP 74
Chapter Six: PARTNERSHIP 104
Chapter Seven: OWNERSHIP 131
Chapter Eight: MANAGEMENTSHIP – Part One 158
Chapter Nine: MANAGEMENTSHIP - Part Two 168
Chapter Ten: CHAMPIONSHIP 204
Chapter Eleven: Time to Set Sail (Epilogue) 217
Bibliography 220

The Arena Trilogy Project - Copyright © 2019, by Richard Spector

All rights reserved. No part of this publication may be reproduced, distributed, or transmitted in any form or by any means, including photocopying, recording, or other electronic or mechanical methods, without the prior written permission of the publisher, except in the case of brief quotations embodied in critical reviews and certain other uses permitted by copyright law. For permission requests, go to www.ArenaTrilogy.com.

The events in this book have been set down to the best of the author's ability, although some names, timelines and details have been changed to protect the privacy of individuals. Additionally, while the stories you are about to read are based on true events, some of the conversions and situations are docudramatic to enhance the purpose and message of the book.

"Ultimately, leadership is not about glorious crowning acts. It's about keeping your team focused on a goal and motivated to do their best to achieve it, especially when the stakes are high, and the consequences really matter. It is about laying the groundwork for others' success, and then standing back and letting them shine."

— Chris Hadfield, Astronaut and former Commander of the International Space Station

Acknowledgements

Firstly, I'd like to thank my wife Sharon for her unrivaled belief in me and the never-ending support and encouragement throughout this entire writing process. Because of this and all you do; I owe you the world. I only hope you can settle with my unconditional love.

I'd also like to thank Dr. Phillip M. Randall, Executive Coach / Human Capital Consultant, and Managing Partner at The Thorndyke Group. What started out as a brief meeting at Tampa International Airport just over a year ago to discuss the content my first book, has developed into an invaluable professional relationship. Thank you so much for your guidance and mentorship.

Thank you to Angie at Pro-eBook Covers for your amazing work. You put your heart and soul into every book cover design, and it shows. Thank you!

Lastly to my readers, I give my most sincere thank you for taking a chance on me. The Executive Arena was my first attempt at becoming an author, and though I was a nobody, still you took a chance and gave me a shot when you purchased my book. Fast forward almost two years later, here you are standing by me with words of encouragement through messages of anticipation and excitement for this book's release. All I can say is, thank you, thank you, thank you.

Foreword

The Leadership Arena, Mastering the Art of Leadership Through SHIP-building™ and Other Secrets to Individual and Organizational Success is the second product in the trilogy series by Richard Spector. Without question, this edition of the trilogy on leadership presents the most foundational and critical task of effective leadership today, relationship construction. It socializes the basic activities of shipbuilding which are to fertilize and cultivate relationships with those who report to you, those who you report to, and those you associate with as peers.

In this refreshing and practical address, Richard Spector captures and catapults the very essence of the process of leadership through skillful storytelling and the apt injection of nautical metaphor. In the first edition of this unfolding trilogy, Richard Spector advanced the kingship of the arena by placing the responsibility for leadership in the executive suite. The second book in the trilogy introduces the ingredients for effective execution of that leadership process.

While there is so much said about the 'how to' of leadership in literature both seminal and current, this edition provides a Brigade de Cuisine's recipe for successful leadership irrespective of the challenge and warrants a serious and deliberate read for those in pursuit of becoming an effective leader.

-Phillip M. Randall, PhD
International Corporate Speaker and Executive Coach
Managing Partner, The Thorndyke Group
Atlanta, Ga.

Introduction

Though I had walked this corridor hundreds of times, I did so very cautiously as the darkness almost completely blinded me. At 0440 (4:40 AM), the only glimpse of light to help navigate my steps was an outside streetlamp significantly dimmed by the frosting-condensation buildup on the inside of the barrack's windows. This frost was due to the freezing temperatures outside. The weather in January at Recruit Training Command (RTC) Great Lakes Illinois was no laughing matter. As far north of Chicago as you can go without actually entering Wisconsin, the naval base was stationed right on the coast of Lake Michigan.

You see, not long after the Spanish-American war in 1902, the US Navy noticed that many of their best sailors came from the Midwest. So, it was proposed, why not have the training center in that same part of the country? What? Train sailors over a thousand miles away from any ocean? As far-fetched as it seemed, Recruit Training Command Great Lakes was conceived in 1905 under President Roosevelt's leadership, and became fully operational, graduating its first class of 300 sailors in 1911 under President William Howard Taft, his predecessor. While other naval recruit training locations came to pass over time, including Orlando, Florida and

San Diego, California, all were eventually shut down, with the exception of RTC Great Lakes. So, as strange as it sounds, at the time of writing this book, all US Navy Sailors, men and women, are now trained in the Midwest, at RTC Great Lakes, Illinois, hundreds of miles away from any ocean.

A Navy barracks has two rows of beds, which consisted of 25 bunk beds (50 racks) on each side of the compartment, for a total of 100, with lockers for storage situated perfectly in between each bunk. Four small square tables, each with four metal chairs, were strategically placed down the center of the compartment, evenly spaced between the two rows of bunks. Hollywood has done an excellent job of replicating a recruit barracks in many movies. From the humorous Stripes with Bill Murray to the more serious films like Full Metal Jacket and An Officer and a Gentleman, the military Recruit barracks hasn't changed much at all, regardless of the branch of service.

With no tall buildings or mountains to block mother nature from blowing you a kiss, the windchill factor on some nights at Great Lakes could easily reach sixty to eighty degrees below zero. This night was no different. As expected, I could make out the silhouette of an individual standing watch at the end of the hall. He carried the title of Compartment Watch, charged with standing guard over the barracks while the other recruits slept. He stood motionless at parade rest (a relaxed but alert stance) with his M1 rifle at his right side, the butt touching the floor next to his right foot. At the same time, the weapon leaned straight out at an angle with his right hand securely positioned at the top of the handguard, just below the Barrel.

The smell inside almost every building at Recruit Training Command was as unique as it was memorable. The only way to describe it is a combination of fresh paint, floor wax, new uniforms, and body odor. It was not a bad body odor, for instance, if someone didn't shower for a month (because recruits showered daily), it was just an odor of human. Overall, I guess you can say it was like entering a World War One or World War Two barracks that had been well kept and renovated numerous times because that's exactly what it was.

As I slowly approached the compartment watch, he took notice of my presence through his peripheral vision. He immediately turned to my direction, bringing his M1 rifle across his chest at a 45-degree angle, and firmly ordered in a shouting whisper, "Halt! Who goes there?" I stopped and replied sarcastically, "Who the hell do you think it is, Rick?" I could hear the slight smile in his voice as, according to proper procedures, he replied, "Advanced to be recognized!" Rick wasn't his name. In fact, I had no idea who was currently standing watch as it was still too dark to make out a face. Rick was a slang word used by Company Commanders (the Navy's version of a Drill Instructor) and was short for Recruit. We called everyone Rick, regardless of who you were, at least for the first four to six weeks of recruit training before we would begin to recognize each Recruit by name. This particular company was in its seventh week, just days away from graduation. This is why my 'Rick' comment was perceived as humorous, just as I intended. If this were week one or two in recruit training, I wouldn't dare make light of the situation; however, this was not the case. Today was an exceptional day for this company, and I needed them at their best.

As I drew closer to the Compartment Watch, we both almost simultaneously recognized each other. He immediately went to attention, and sounded off: "Sir, Seaman Recruit Zimmerman, Company 077, all present and accounted for, Sir!" I never responded immediately after a recruit sounded off, in part for effect, but mostly just to keep the Recruit guessing on what I was going to do or ask next. Also, while standing at attention, you were allowed to speak and answer any questions I may have, something you were not allowed to do in the Parade Rest position. I stepped just pass the Compartment Watch so he couldn't see my face. "So, Zimmerman, am I to assume everyone is sound asleep in their bunks?" I asked with a smile while staring out over the sea of racks (bunk Beds) that stretched out into the darkness. "Yes, Sir," he replied confidently. I turned to look at Zimmerman. "And no one has gotten out of their bunks for any reason this morning?" I asked for clarification. "No, sir, not to my knowledge," he replied. As soon as he said that, I could hear a gurgling sound coming from my office. The Company Commander's office was situated just behind where the Compartment Watch would stand guard at the front of the barracks. As I leaned my head over to look past Zimmerman and into my office, I noticed a red-glowing light illuminating a small table where my coffee pot sat. The now-familiar gurgling sound was an indication that the coffee brewing cycle was approaching completion. I turned back to look at Zimmerman, who was now trying his best not to express his nervousness. "And no one has been in my office, either?" I asked, full knowing what his response would be. "Not to my knowledge Sir." He said.

'Fucking King,' I thought to myself, with a slight smile of approval as I shook my head. King was the company Yeoman. The "Yeoman" was a recruit leadership position (one of about 10) that was assigned extra duties to assist in managing the company. The Yeoman, much like an Executive Assistant, was by far the most critical position to a Company Commander, along with the RPOC or Recruit Chief Petty Officer. In our absence, the Yeoman knew what needed to be done and where the recruits needed to be, and the RPOC knew how to get them there.

King knew the importance of today and knew how much I would want a hot cup of coffee first thing in the morning. Thus, he took it upon himself to get up early and get the coffee brewing before I arrived to wake the company. Of course, it was against regulations to be up before reveille was sounded (Reveille is a French word meaning Wake Up); however, it was unwritten, or I guess you can say, an accepted practice when the situation deemed it necessary. Furthermore, it was my guess that while the other recruits 'appeared' to be snuggled all nicely in their bunks, they were, in fact, already fully dressed, just waiting for the moment I turned on the lights to wake them. Today you see was their final barracks inspection before graduation, which would also include a locker inspection back to back. So, we needed to be up, dressed, out the door, and at the Chow Hall (dining facility) as soon as possible, so we could quickly eat and get back to prepare for inspection. Time was of the essence, and it seemed the recruits already knew this.

This company, Company 077, was unique. You see, each company had two Company Commanders, and for the first time in naval history, two brothers were training companies together. My brother and I would train this company and go on to teach another as well, but it wasn't easy getting permission to serve together, let alone work as partners. We had to interview with leadership and convince them we would be successful even during a family emergency should one arise. Additionally, because of this rare occasion, all eyes were on this company and its performance. They also did a story on us in the Great Lakes Bulletin, (the local base newspaper) titled "Brothers in Arms." While this all sounded like a great idea in the beginning, "making naval history" and all, we quickly realized our fifteen minutes of fame came at a price not fair to the recruits we were leading. This added publicity, unfortunately, came with additional scrutiny and higher expectations in recruit performance. The powers at be were watching because if we failed, there would surely be regulations written against allowing

The Leadership Arena

family or any kind of nepotism into the ranks of Company Commanders for the foreseeable future. However, that said, we didn't care about our reputations as Company Commanders or CC's as we were called for short; our careers were doing fine. What we truly cared about was the success of these recruits. Because of no fault of their own, they had to be the best. Because of this situation, they had to look sharper, and do it better than their counterparts in other companies. Believe me; no one was cutting them any slack because they were part of the "Brothers in Arms" company.

"Are we ready, Zimmerman?" I asked as I turned to face him, noticing he was still standing at attention. He replied with a proud smile, "Yes, Sir!" I leaned over to the row of eight light switches on the wall and began to flick them on two at a time. Starting from the rear of the barracks moving towards us in sections, the compartment lit up in both light, movement, and sound. As I had expected, as each blanket was turned back, up jumped a recruit fully dressed and ready to go. I walked into my office, turned on the light, poured myself a cup of coffee, and stood to gaze at the company through the large picture window that faced out at the long rows of bunks. They operated like a well-tuned machine. Just seven weeks ago, I would be tossing trash cans, yelling out orders, instructing them on what to do and when to do it. But not today. All I did was turn on the lights, stood back, and watched as the magic happened.

Richard Spector

As I stood sipping my coffee, I pondered the fact that most probably assume graduation day is one of the proudest or most gratifying moments for a Company Commander. But honestly, for me, it's wasn't. Graduation is important, don't get me wrong, but it's essential for the recruits. It's their day to shine. It's a day they mark as the completion of something important, and for most recruits, it just might be the most significant achievement in their lives up to that point. To them, it's the day they became a Sailor. But for me, today is when I am filled with gratitude. Today is when I feel the most satisfaction. Today, when I look out over the barracks and notice, with the single flick of a switch, this company, this team, this family, is operating all on their own. In less than two months, they have formed friendships, built relationships, and forged partnerships. They have witnessed and experienced the ingredients of authentic leadership and embraced the power of mentorship.

In summary, they now have a solid foundation towards mastering the Art of Leadership through SHIP-building™ and, hopefully, will continue to build upon that foundation. Today is when I'm most proud. Today is when they indeed became Sailors. Graduation Day is merely a date chosen to advertise that fact to the public.

So, you might be wondering, why would I start a book about leadership with a story about recruit training or "Boot Camp." Let's face it, Hollywood has painted a pretty good picture that recruit training is all about being a good follower, right? Just shut up and do what you're told, and if you make a mistake, you'll surely be rewarded with more push-ups than you can literally count. And I'm sure some of you have heard the rumors or claims that boot camp brainwashes you, and the military only wants obedient robots to carry out its missions. Well, I assure you, from someone who has not only been through boot camp as a recruit but has gone back as a CC and pushed (trained) nine companies, it's simply not true. Ok, the push-up thing might have some truth to it, I'll admit that. But let me explain why sharing this experience with you is so vital in properly introducing this book.

For centuries, the military has known that the best way to train someone is to expose them to situations they may face in the future. In other words, you can't just watch training films or take college courses and expect to become a great leader. When you are exposed to actual situations, even in training, you are better prepared when faced with like conditions in the future. It's kind of a "been there, done that" preparedness. This type of training modality is called conditioning. This is why having a confidante (as discussed in my last book, The Executive Arena) early in one's career is essential in the corporate world because they, most times, have the experience, not just the knowledge you may need at a given moment.

Furthermore, this conditioning style of learning, more often than not, might be teaching you valuable lessons of which you are not even aware. For example, remember the original movie The Karate Kid with Ralph Macchio? The whole "sand the floor" and "paint the fence" thing were perfect examples of the conditioning modality. The character Daniel, (Mr. Miyagi's student), didn't even realize what Mr. Miyagi was teaching him, until far into his training. Making him paint his fence, using specific strokes with the paintbrush, and hand-sand his entire wooden deck, with no questions asked, was, in fact, a style of conditioning. Yes, that type of training does exist. As a real-life example, let's go back to boot camp and the upcoming locker inspection I spoke about previously.

During a locker inspection, the recruits will have 60 seconds to empty their lockers and unfold every piece of clothing they have and place it in piles on their bunks. This includes all their uniforms, underwear, T-shirts, everything, even their jackets, and raincoats. Once that is complete, the recruits then have 12 minutes, to refold everything and place it properly back into the locker, in accordance with navy regulations. During this time, as the minutes are counted down out loud, the recruits are being evaluated by an inspector, which everyone calls MED an acronym for Military Evaluation Division. They are basically other Company Commanders taking a break in between pushing companies. (Trust me, after training three companies in a row, you need a break). Once the 12 minutes are up, the recruits then stand at attention in front of their bunks, while MED and the Company Commanders inspect each locker. If a recruit receives a Hit (infraction) because something was not folded correctly, or placed improperly in the locker, rest assured push-ups and other strenuous exercises would be in every

Recruit's future. Additionally, each infraction would be counted against the company's overall score as a team.

Now, keep that inspection in mind, and ask yourself, what is the lesson being taught here? Why do they have to fold their clothes properly, and place them a certain way in their lockers? I actually did a few surveys while stationed at RTC Great lakes and ask hundreds of recruits that very question, among others. While I received a lot of different answers, most seemed to respond with "There is limited storage space on a ship" and "Attention to detail", or "It builds teamwork". While all of these responses have some truth, they are not the most important lesson being taught here. Again, locker inspections are a form of conditioning. Here is the real lesson: It takes six steps to fold a Navy issued t-shirt properly. If a recruit cannot remember those simple six steps under pressure, and by pressure, I mean time constraints and being judged by a superior, how will he/she be able to follow the 12 steps necessary to fire a missile in a real-life situation? How will they remember the procedure to properly don (put on) firefighting gear in an emergency?

The locker inspection was meant to teach recruits how to think clearly and function properly under pressure. Exposure to as many of these situations as possible better prepares them for the future and opens the door for further learning as they advance in their naval careers. Additionally, conditioning helps with retention when learning new material, and that is what I intend to do for you! In this book, The Leadership Arena, Mastering the

Art of Leadership Through SHIP-building™ and Other Secrets to Individual and Organizational Success, I will not be pushing leadership theories. I will not be merely listing the tons of 'success strategies', or 'leadership principles' or other "keys to success" that have been written or talked about repeatedly. Instead, my goal is to expose you through the concept of SHIP-building™ to as many real-life situations as possible. To instill in you, through conditioning, the values, and behaviors of a true leader, the concepts that have worked time and time again, and the tactics employed that promote both individual and organizational success. Some of the stories you will read may be short, while others are a bit longer, but just know they are all based on actual events and designed to help you experience the lesson, not just read about it.

You see, real leadership is not about being the shining star or the hero. It's not about making a name for yourself or 'being a good boss'. As Astronaut Chris Hadfield once said, leadership is "…laying the groundwork for others' success, and then standing back and letting them shine." So, let's turn the pages together and explore Part-two of the Arena Trilogy, The Leadership Arena.

Chapter One: What is *SHIP-Building*™?

As I stepped out of my car and swung my sea bag over my shoulder, I looked up and gazed towards the direction of my first real job out of high school. It had been only five months since I enlisted in the Navy, and so much had already been accomplished. I had just completed Navy boot camp and initial training (something the Navy calls A-School) and was given orders a few days after graduation to report to my first ship. There, about a half-mile away from where I was, stood the biggest ship I had ever seen! Off in the distance was the U.S.S. Forrestal CV-59, an aircraft carrier commissioned back in 1955, 10 years before I was even born. It was the world's first "Super-Carrier," which meant it had four catapults to launch planes (along with an angled deck) versus its predecessors, which only had two. This being 1983, the ship now 28 years old, she was in dire need of an overhaul, which is exactly what was going on. While my first assignment was to be on-board a ship (classified as sea duty), she was stationed at the Philadelphia Naval Shipyards going through what the Navy called "SLEP" or the Ships Life Extension Program.

As I began the trek across the hot and vast parking lot towards the ship, I noticed a large white van labeled 'Parking Shuttle,' slowly approaching a makeshift bus stop. By makeshift, I mean a metal sign reading "Shuttle" bolted to a small steel pole, that was sunk in a 5-gallon bucket of concrete. I quickly picked up my pace to catch the shuttle and climbed in to hitch a ride. As we continued towards the ship, I realized that at each shuttle stop, the higher the level of boarding passengers. It soon became apparent that the higher your military rank, the closer to the ship you could park. Unbeknownst at the time, the phrase RHIP or "rank has its privileges" would quickly become commonplace in the Navy.

As the shuttle arrived at its final destination, the other passengers and I quickly grabbed our things and stepped out of the van. It was there, for the first time, I stood face to face with what would be my 'new home' for the next few years. What I thought was big while viewing her from a half-mile away, was now absolutely enormous! This ship towered over 20 stories high from the waterline and was easily over 1000 feet long and nearly 250 feet wide. To put it in perspective, if you lifted the Forrestal straight up, she would be about the same height as the Chrysler Building in New York, and about 150 feet shy of equaling the Empire State Building. I was in awe and speechless, proud, and intimidated all at the same time. "How could something that huge, made of solid steel even float?" I remember thinking to myself. Then came the biggest surprise of all. As I began to walk towards the guardrails that surrounded the doc, I heard and saw the sounds of banging steel and bright lights flickering from welding torches. With each step closer, more of the ship's hull became visible, and I soon realized the ship wasn't

The Leadership Arena

floating in the water at all. She was in drydock! Once I reached the guardrail, I looked down. It was an image that will remain burned into my memory forever. Not only was there just as much ship below the waterline as there was above, the most essential elements in its construction were now visible.

The Keel is the backbone of the ship and the foundation on which all else is built upon. Stretching fore and aft (from front to back), the entire Keel was supported by close to 100 large concrete and steel blocks, which by some engineering marvel, held the whole ship off the ground. Four bronze propellers, each weighing about 30 tons and over 20 feet in diameter, peered out from the bottom of the hull. Dozens of shipyard personnel worked diligently and moved about on hundreds of yards of scaffolding that surrounded the ship's hull. It was an incredible sight to see for a new sailor barely 19 years old. However, I learned an invaluable lesson that day.

The term SHIP-building™ as it relates to the subtitle of this book was created for two important reasons, one of which was the lesson I learned on that very first day at the Shipyards. Let me explain.

1. When you experience real Leadership, it will come in all shapes and sizes and from a wide range of industries. From corporate executives to football coaches, from military personnel to entrepreneurs, one's profession and leadership style will vary greatly. Like all naval ships - their form, purpose, and the tools they will utilize will

differ depending on what they need to accomplish. Moreover, as with both shipbuilding and Leadership, some elements are fundamental and essential - unchanging. Both must be built precisely and with the proper parts to be successful. Every ship must be made with a sturdy Keel, the backbone or foundation on which the rest of the vessel is built. From there, the hull is produced, followed by Decks and Bulkheads (floors and walls) that form Compartments. Each compartment is designed to fulfill a specific role or purpose.

Mastering the Art of Leadership through SHIP-building™ involves laying down a strong Keel or foundation on which other essential elements of leadership extend from and are built upon. We will talk about these key elements in detail as we progress through this book.

2. The second reason I used the term SHIP-building™ was because of each specific 'leadership element' that is present in all great leaders. Take the word Leadership, for example. The suffix of this word is "-ship." That same suffix, coincidentally, is also present in each of the leadership elements we will be discussing. From Partnership and Directorship to Mentorship and Studentship, it was clear the term SHIP-building™ was the best decision in presenting the book's theme and direction.

We will discuss in detail the key elements to Mastering the Art of Leadership Through SHIP-building™ and Other Secrets to Individual and Organizational Success as we progress through the following pages. However, before we discuss how to transform into a great leader, we must first dispel some myths and spend a little time considering what Leadership is NOT.

Chapter Two: What Leadership is NOT.

Management vs. Leadership - *It's not that Difficult!*

I climbed aboard the commuter train at Main Street Station in McHenry, Illinois, and took a seat on the lower level. I took off my coat, hat, and gloves and set them next to me on the bench seat. I got comfortable as it would take about an hour and a half (at least) to reach downtown Chicago. About 30 minutes into the ride, as I glanced over my newspaper not seeing anything of interest, I couldn't help but overhear a couple's conversion from across the aisle.

"Sarah is a great manager," the man exclaimed. "She really understands when I'm late or if I have to call out for the day." "Wow," responded the woman. "I wish I had a boss like that. If I were late or had to call off, Jerry would have my butt. He's such a poor leader".

While the above conversation is brief, it brings to light a significant point. In today's corporate world, the vast influx of communication technology, social media enterprise, combined with a changing workforce, has significantly changed how we communicate at work. I'm not saying there is less communication; in fact, I believe there is even more communication now than ever! However, the way we communicate, and the quality of communication has changed drastically in a lot of cases. Take the above conversation, for example. In a quick 10-second conversation, the words management and leadership were used interchangeably, which is not an uncommon event.

Think about phrases like "He's a great manager" or "He's such a poor leader." First of all, there is no such thing as a 'poor leader' in my book (no pun intended). If someone can't lead effectively, then they are not a leader at all, are they? Simply put, leaders don't manage people; they lead them. Sure, you can manage employee schedules; you can maintain a budget or P&L, even manage employee benefits or payroll. But when it comes to those in your charge, the human aspect of your job, leaders LEAD!

In an article from Harvard Business Review, titled Three Differences Between Managers and Leaders, Vineet Nayar describes it brilliantly. He writes: "Management consists of controlling a group or a set of entities to accomplish a goal. Leadership refers to an individual's ability to influence, motivate, and enable others to contribute toward organizational success. Influence and inspiration separate leaders from managers, not power and control."

I would add to Mr. Nayar's statement by saying that leadership refers to "one's ability to influence, motivate, and enable others to contribute to organizational and individual success!" Because inspiring someone to improve themselves through personal and professional development is just as crucial as making organizational contributions. We will talk more about this in a later chapter.

In summary, there is a vast difference between management and leadership. Regardless of your profession or industry, you can't allow titles and common business terminology to confuse you. For example, I've seen people on LinkedIn, who've given themselves the claim of Business Leader or Chicago Area Leader in their profile. Having the word 'leader' in a title doesn't denote real leadership. In fact, I think it's a little conceded because real leaders don't purposefully advertise that fact. Lastly, someone at your place of business might be in a "leadership role," but that doesn't mean they are, in fact, leaders. Another colleague may be great at managing payroll, taking care of inventory, or scheduling and hosting some great company functions for all to enjoy. In other words, they complete the tasks required in their job description, and they do so quite well. That in itself may make them a great manager or a good employee, but it does not necessarily make them a leader.

Positional Authority vs. Earned Authority.

David walked into the marketing lab and did a quick scan over the room to ensure everyone was present. As the marketing team diligently went about their work, David,

The Leadership Arena

the Director of Advertising, walked over to the conference table that was positioned in the middle of the room and pulled out a chair. 'This would be the best way to speak to everyone,' he thought to himself. But he didn't sit down. David stepped up onto the seat of the chair, giving him an unobstructed view of all 12 marketing team members. "Hey, everyone, can I have your attention for a bit, please?" he started. Each member quickly began to turn around in their chairs, or looked up, closed their laptops, put down their phones, etc., readying themselves to give David the attention he requested. All eyes were upon him now. "I know you have all been working hard over the past two months on this project, but I have a bit of bad news," he stated while raising his hand, placing his forefinger and thumb about an inch apart from each other. "Unfortunately, due to a family emergency, Amy has taken a leave of absence. With that, obviously, she can no longer be your team's Project Leader." The staff briefly looked around at each other, no doubt surprised by the news, but quickly redirected their attention back to David. "So," David continued, "Instead of electing a new project leader myself, I thought it best to let all of you make the decision for me." Again, heads began to turn as if the decision-making process had already started.

"Look, you guys know best how the team works, so I'll give you until the end of the week to decide," said David. "Today is Tuesday, so that gives you about four days to make your decision. Talk amongst yourselves and let me know what you decide on Friday". David stepped down, pushed in the chair, and turned to walk towards the door he had entered initially. Before he could even take two steps, almost in unison, the name "Marcus" rang out from at least three people. David stopped in his tracks, turned around, and said, "Marcus?" "Yes, sir," one of the team members answered. Another jumped in with, "He's always helping everyone out and knows how to keep us all on track." "And he's just awesome to work with," injected a third team member. "I mean, he keeps us inspired and makes it fun!" The other team members nodded in agreement. David, now pleasantly surprised by the outcome of his announcement, looked over at Marcus, lifted his eyebrows forming a 'do you approve?' face. With a smile and a nod from Marcus, David turned and headed for the door and, in a loud voice, confirmed, "Marcus it is!"

So, let's get right to the point. Marcus had developed earned authority, and he wasn't even in a management position. What Marcus did possess is what I like to call the two "I's" in the word " leader. As Mr. Nayar mentioned previously, the "I's" eyes in a leader are Influence and Inspiration.

Every management position comes with its specific level of Positional Authority. As the phrase denotes, it comes with the job. For example, a Service Manager at an automotive dealership may have the authority to hire and fire mechanics and other administrative staff needed in his/her department. A Director of Shipping may have the power to purchase up to $15,000 a month in supplies without any further approval. These are all examples of Positional Authority, and it "comes with the territory" for lack of better words. While positional authority is required and frankly a necessary element in any leadership position, on its own, it is constrained. It will only take you and your team so far.

As you might have already concluded, Earned Authority is the authority you have earned from your team, or others around you, because you inspire others! You influence those around you to think outside the box, or to be more creative - to do more! In the example above, the team members truly enjoyed working with Marcus. They would come to him for advice or help, and because of his leading by example, he inspired them, and the team, in turn, developed a great respect for Marcus. That is Earned Authority. When you genuinely possess earned authority, your team and even members outside your team, want to work for you. They want to do things for you, even without you asking. And above all, they do not want to disappoint you.

CRITICAL NOTE: Real leaders understand that the control you are granted through Positional Authority might bring you a few doors of opportunity, but Earned Authority will kick them wide-open every time!

Leaders are Born vs. Leaders are Made

Are leaders born or made? I'm sorry, but I can't believe this question is still being asked and debated. It has been posed time and time again, and I can't help but laugh at the witlessness and vast opinions for one side or the other. The question is posted on social media sites, talked about in articles, and even posed in various college courses and other formal venues even today in the year 2020. So, once and for all, let me give you the definitive answer so that we can move on with the more critical topics and lessons in this book. LEADERS ARE MADE! Period.

Let's look at this from a commonsense perspective. If leaders were born, why would anyone read this book? Why are you? Why would you go out and read any of the hundreds of thousands of leadership books that have been available since the invention of the printing press? Why spend your hard-earned money on even a single college course on leadership development, or pay for a seminar on how to enhance your leadership skills? I mean, if leaders were born, the military would be in serious trouble, because they depend, survive, and strive on enhanced leadership abilities by a vast majority of their ranks. You see, I believe this crazy question all started with a famous phrase we have all heard at one time or another; The phrase "Natural Born Leader." When you hear the term Born Leader, take it for what it is. It's a figure of speech, and it's not meant to be taken literally. When someone calls another a natural-born leader, what they mean is that the person is so good at leading, that they are so good at what they do, they make it look easy. So again, take it for what it is - a figure of speech.

Now, that said, are there specific attributes or a talent someone can be born with that can perhaps give them an advantage in mastering the art of leadership? Of course, however, those attributes still need to be polished and cultivated to be perfected. As a metaphor, it's like playing the piano or any musical instrument. There are those that can play an instrument "by ear." It means, for example, one can listen to a song on the radio, and after about 5 minutes of trial and error, it can be played on the piano or keyboard almost perfectly. They can't read music, nor have they had music lessons. That example would be classified as a talent one was born with. However, anyone can take piano lessons, and in a few short years, (if not sooner) could surely surpass the ladder in skills and ability.

Additionally, even though one may have an "ear" for music, they would still have to practice for hours to hone the ability and improve. Now imagine, if someone had an "ear" for music and took professional lessons? They would, of course, have an advantage over their counterparts, but the fact remains, and the point still proves… Leaders Are Made.

That said, the final point and a crucial one is this: Just because leaders are made, doesn't mean anyone can be made to be a leader. Unlike the previously used music analogy, it takes a particular personality, combined with specific academic abilities and attributes one must possess to become a great leader. The best analogy I can use is the making of a doctor. I'm sure we can all agree, doctors are made. However, I'm sure we can all equally agree that not everyone that decides to go to medical school will be successful. I mean, I consider myself halfway intelligent on the academic scale, but I know for a fact, I'm not doctor material.

Millennials vs. today's workforce

This chapter would not be complete, and I would be remiss if we didn't talk about one trendy buzzword, which frankly is a hot point for me. Whether you are 25 or 65 years old, or somewhere in between, this is a critical lesson that will prove extremely beneficial in mastering the art of leadership. This buzzword and its surrounding business topics have made their way into the mainstream media, books, magazines, and professional blogs alike. The word is Millennials. It's a topic as big as the Keto diet, and publishers, social media companies and other organizations are cashing in on its popularity. Hey, it's a great way to make a buck. Just do a google search for two simple words, Millennials and Workforce, and watch the hundreds of thousands of results that will surface. The messages being disseminated relate to such topics as "What millennials want from their managers" or "When dealing with millennials, a new type of leadership is needed" as if leadership as we know it is somehow outdated in some way. These types of topics are fantastic marketing tactics, but they couldn't be further from the truth. I've read these books, and I've read these articles because I, too, strive to remain current in my industry.

The Leadership Arena

What's fascinating is, when it comes to real Leadership, most of the stuff I read was not saying anything new! For example, I read an article titled "What Millennials Need in a Boss" or words to that effect. I don't want to name a publisher of sorts, because I don't believe in badmouthing another author or company. It said in a nutshell; Millennials want to be "appreciated, mentored, and inspired." That they needed their bosses to be "good listeners, coaching, understanding and not afraid to get their hands dirty." Um, hello? Do you see my point here? That's not just what Millennials want; that's what every good employee wants, and it's what real leadership strives to provide! If you genuinely understand leadership, then you know there is no "special way" of leading millennials or any other generation.

So why is this happening? Well, aside from the money-making angle mentioned previously, it's really quite simple. It's a matter of perception. Sadly, the number of managers in today's workforce dramatically outweighs the amount of real leaders among them. In short, authentic leadership is hard to come by, and always will be. For example, take an intelligent 25-year-old (millennial) aspiring executive who happens to be working for a crappy boss in his 60's, (baby boomer) and the wrong conclusion can quickly be drawn. It's easy to associate that bad boss's "leadership style" as an old-outdated way of doing things. The fact of the matter is, the crappy boss was not exuding any real leadership at all. He was just a lousy boss, and in the absence of genuine leadership, it's only natural for a young aspiring executive to assume what he is experiencing is some form of leadership. Well, it's not. Nevertheless, the association has been made and now widely publicized. Unfortunately, this misinformation only leads to more negative generalizations between different generations.

Lastly, because of the positive advances in technology and an ever-changing, more family-based culture, the corporate working environment has changed drastically, and I believe for the better. The days of windowless rooms full of 6-foot tall cubicles and business-dressed work-a-bees are quickly being replaced with open "no-walls" team atmospheres, filled with jeans and sandals and "bring your pet" workdays. Working remotely from a satellite location or even from home is becoming more commonplace, not to mention things like extended maternity leave for both parents! So yes, the working environment in today's corporate world has changed drastically; however, the elements of real leadership have not.

> CRITICAL NOTE: Today's working generation we call Millennials is a fantastic group of intelligent, creative, tolerant, and caring people. And as with all current and future generations, whether you like it or not, they are and will become the future leaders of this world. So, we can continue to generalize and patronize the different generations, or we can come together, learn together, and help lead them to success.

The Leadership Arena

Through SHIP-building™, we will cover the elements that are time-tested, unchanged, and critical to your success as a leader. First, we will lay the Keel - the most crucial foundation, then continue building the other vital compartments until we've completed your leadership vessel. Then, all you have to do is set sail!

Chapter Three: MENTORSHIP – Laying the Keel

"Great Leaders Don't Try to be Heroes, They Strive to Create Them."

"Are you crazy?" whispered Smith, ensuring his voice remained below acceptable chow-hall levels. "How are you going to make three bunks in the allotted time?" "Yeah, we're screwed," Jones added. Ryan quickly looked at Jones, placing his forefinger in front of his lips, reminding both to keep their voices down. In Bootcamp, while recruits were allowed to talk at chow (mealtime), it was at a volume equivalent to a heavy whisper and only while seated at a table.

With anywhere from five hundred to eight hundred recruits eating at one time, the noise level could quickly get out of hand otherwise. "Look," Smith said to Ryan, "Jones and I suck at making our bunks. We just can't get those hospital corners right. So just let it go, and if we fail, we will take whatever punishment we get, including going to IT." Ryan could sense they were ready to give up.

The Leadership Arena

IT stood for Intensive Training. It was where recruits would go to pay for their mistakes when the Company Commander deemed the error serious enough. Mistakes were things like failing a bunk inspection or academic exam, or even marching out of step should the CC be in a shitty mood that day. Recruits sent to IT would muster (assemble) in a designated drill hall, which literally looked like an enormous world war two airplane hangar. This training would happen at night around 8 PM and would not end until well after TAPS or Lights-out. It consisted of over two-hours of intensive exercise, with your M1 rifle in hand. This spectacle was directed and highly enjoyed by numerous Company Commanders working a night shift. From sit-ups and leg lifts to running in place, while lifting your rifle up and down over your head, were just some of the "corrective measures" a recruit would endure. It was something no recruit ever wanted to experience, and something you'd never forget, should you be granted the privilege. When finished, the recruits were sent back to their company, exhausted, with uniforms entirely soaked in sweat, tears even vomit, or a combination of all three.

Ryan leaned in to draw closer attention from Smith and Jones. "This is what we will do," Ryan began to explain. "During the bunk inspection this afternoon, I will make my bunk as fast as possible, and you guys do the same. Once I get my bunk done, I will tap you…" he pointed to Smith, "on the shoulder when the inspector is not looking. When I do, you switch to work on my bunk, and I'll work on yours. I will fix your hospital corners, and you pretend to be working on my bunk. It's easy because you sleep right above me, and the inspector doesn't know whose bunk belongs to who." Smith nodded in agreement. Ryan turned his head to Jones. "Then when I'm finished, I'll do yours. Same thing, a single tap on the shoulder. Agreed?" Ryan asked for confirmation. "Oh, and one more thing," Ryan injected. "Once we get passed this, let's all agree to use whatever free time we get to practice for future inspections. I'll show you how I do it, okay?" Fist bumps sealed the deal.

As the inspection concluded, the MED inspector tore off the top sheet of his inspection pad and handed it to the company commander. With a nod and a handshake, the inspector made his way to the exit as the Company Commander stared at the results in his hand. The recruits all stood at attention in front of their bunks, both nervous and anxious to hear the results. After what seemed like forever, the Company Commander finally looked up from staring at the results and tossed the report into the air. The paper, gliding side to side, slowly floated down towards the deck before coming to rest in front of his feet. No one dared to look in his direction as they prepared for the worst. "I have some good news," he began. "To date, this has been the best bunk inspection results we have received." You could almost see the tension being released from the recruit's bodies as some of their faces began to light up with slight smiles, though they didn't dare leave the position of attention. "However, we did have one person fail the inspection, and honestly, this failure comes as a surprise," he continued. "So, instead of punishing everyone for this stupid mistake, tonight he will go to IT and pay for his lack of attention to detail." All the smiles, as mentioned earlier, disappeared. "Will the following recruit please step forward," he ordered. Five seconds of complete silence was followed by the words "Seaman Recruit Ryan!" As Ryan slowly and precisely took one step forward, both Smith and Jones closed their eyes in disbelief, for they had passed the inspection with Ryan's help. Nevertheless, Ryan would pay for their success.

Mentorship is the KEEL of your leadership vessel. It is the foundation, and by far, the most critical element in mastering the art of leadership. Just as with actual shipbuilding, if you don't have a sturdy keel, the rest of the ship doesn't matter. When building a house, you need a strong foundation, or regardless of the quality of materials used, it could come crashing down. If you were to only take away one critical lesson from this book, then this should be it, hands down. If I were to describe the true meaning of Mentorship in a single sentence, it would be the following: 'Great Leaders Don't Try to be Heroes, They Strive to <u>Create</u> Them.' The Ryan story helps unearth several crucial lessons relating to Mentorship. Ryan, even though he was not officially in any management or leadership position, knew deep down inside that he had to help his shipmates if they were to be successful as a team. Not only did he want them to pass the inspection, but he was also willing to give up his free time to mentor them going forward. Ryan was showing real leadership in its most raw form, not once considering or worrying about his reputation or the possibility of failing the inspection. He was willing to take the risk for the betterment of the team.

Regardless of your current position, title, or even the bullet points in your job description, your number one priority should be <u>to ensure those in your charge are successful</u>, hard stop! Whether you're a director, a vice president of operations, or a shift supervisor at your local retail store, your focus should always be on the success of those in your charge. It's your job to ensure your people have all the tools, training, and guidance necessary to be successful in their position. Do that, practice that, and in turn, you will be successful. Unfortunately, too many times, even the most experienced executives forget that fact. They get lost worrying about their own reputation and the possible kudos they might earn in the future. I'm not saying you shouldn't want to be successful or have the desire to become a very successful leader; of course, you should. We should all want to succeed and be proud of our achievements as we continue to improve and strive for excellence. But how you get there, how you become a great leader starts by focusing on the success of those around you, not your own!

Again, Mentorship is the Keel or foundation on which all other leadership elements are built upon and is the lifeblood of a great leader. Even as a Doctor, while your purpose is to provide the best healthcare possible for your patients, you can't do that unless your nurses are top-notch and successful themselves. I heard a great quote that has stuck with me for years that really drives home this point. Okay, to be fair, I heard it from a nurse, but it still carries a lot of truth. 'Doctors diagnose; Nurses heal!' So, remember, like a ship rises and falls with the tide, if those in your charge are successful, you, in turn, will be successful as well.

Lead Now, Get Promoted Later

Another lesson we can extract from the Ryan story is you don't have to be in a leadership role to be a leader. Ryan and even Marcus, from chapter two, both displayed leadership elements long before they were in an official leadership position. What I haven't revealed to you yet about the Ryan story, was the fact that Smith and Jones did confess to the company commander about how Ryan had helped them pass inspection. Even though Ryan still had to go to IT because he failed the inspection, he was soon promoted to Squad Leader, so he could officially continue to mentor Smith, Jones, and the other recruits in his squad. In both cases, they were promoted, not because they were superstars at their job, but because they were performing as a leader. Through Mentorship, they both gained influence and inspired others. These leadership elements are also why I have repeated the following statement to many sales leaders during coaching sessions: "A great salesman won't necessarily make a great sales manager, " which brings me to another important lesson about Mentorship.

Mentorship and Sales Management

Whether you are in sales or not, it is vitally important you understand how Mentorship, being the Keel of your leadership vessel, is also a guiding principle to becoming a great leader over those who are actually in sales and sales management. We will be discussing some of the following in more detail in an upcoming chapter; however, we need to touch on a few critical elements as they relate heavily to Mentorship. Additionally, if you have any desire to enter senior management someday or lead an entire organization, you need to be familiar with the ingredients of a sales environment. You should be aware that most presidents and CEOs today have some (if not extensive) experience in sales and sales management. Most have risen through the ranks from, or through sales positions before finally being promoted into senior management. But that doesn't mean you have to come from a sales background to be a successful leader or become the President or CEO of an organization. However, you should be able to comprehend the concepts and maneuvers required as a leader within the sales arena. While this next section could be a book all in itself (and perhaps it will be someday), there are a few elements we need to cover as it relates to Mentorship and Sales Management.

<u>Diamonds in the Rough:</u> Adi was one of the best instructors I had ever experienced. I had recently been hired as an Applications Instructor for a computer training company in Chicago. I needed to audit several computer training classes before they would allow me to teach on

my own. If I remember correctly, Adi was the third instructor I was auditing, and his class was the most enjoyable I had ever attended. What I remember the most about his teaching style was how creative and animated he was. This class was not the type of computer training I was used to attending. We were laughing, joking, and sometimes we would even stop to discuss a particular student's situation at work and the struggles they were having with their computer software. I mean, it looked the instructor was having so much fun that he was neglecting the actual lesson plan. But I was wrong. Adi was following the instructor's outline for the class exactly! The students were so engaged and inspired by Adi's method of teaching; they didn't even realize just how much they were learning. Hell, I didn't realize we were "learning" at all. From my perspective, we were just having a great time.

The point here is this: Adi was called into the General Manager's office just a few short weeks after our class and offered a promotion. However, it was not the promotion one might expect. The General Manager, whose name was Robert at the time, was so impressed with the way Adi could inspire and motivate those in his charge, he was offered the position of Sales Manager. Yes, you read that correctly – an Instructor was asked to become the sales manager. Of course, Adi's initial response was, "No way, I hate selling, and I don't really have any sales management experience!" After some meaningful discussions, Adi accepted the position and, with proper mentoring, went on to be a successful Sales

Manager. Now, I would be lying if I told you he was welcomed warmly with open arms by the sales team. Many sales reps, especially the senior ones, initially had a hard time respecting him as a leader. However, Adi being the person he was, continued to charge forward, and soon earned their respect. Adi was a diamond in the rough and, with genuine mentoring, became a great leader.

You see, I've heard time and time again a belief that the next logical step for a top sales rep should be sales management. Similarly, if someone is looking for a sales manager, one of the typical requirements is that he/she should be one of the top sales reps. But this belief, while widely practiced is just not true, because the skills required for success in each position are very different. Successful sales reps are great presenters, problem solvers, relationship builders, and above all, great closers! Successful sales managers are motivators, influencers, team builders, and, most of all, coaches and mentors. The skillset of these two positions are exceedingly dissimilar, yet it happens all the time. It happens because, quite frankly, it's the easiest decision - the easy way out, with little to no training needed. Decision-makers assume that all the top salesperson has to do, is teach the other sales reps to be top salespeople - to do what he/she did. But it doesn't work that way.

In short, always be on the lookout for the diamond in the rough, even across teams, departments, companies, or industries. Because with Mentorship, you have the tools to polish, coach, and nurture tomorrow's amazing leaders.

<u>The Weakest Link Deserves Your Attention:</u> When Mentorship is not the priority, a lot of managers fall victim to what I call the "bailout syndrome." Let me explain. The following can happen whether you're in sales or not. Any department or division manager that has an important project to complete or deadline to meet can fall victim to the bailout syndrome. For the sake of simplicity, let's use a sales manager, for example. It's the 25th of the month, and the sales manager is seriously worried about hitting his department's monthly sales goal only five days away. A couple of sales fell through, one got delayed unexpectedly, and now the reality of missing his target is taking its toll. He needs to do whatever he can to reach that goal, or this will be a red mark on his record. What does he do? Answer: He goes to his top performers and applies pressure. He tells them things like, "I really need you to pull off another sale," and "the team needs you; I know you can find some new business in the next few days." Well, as luck would have it, the top producers do what they do best, and the team hits their goal! The sales manager is feeling great having avoided the embarrassment, or worse written up for missing a monthly sales goal. He's in the clear, for now.

The problem with this scenario is two-fold. Firstly, you may be thinking to yourself, 'hey, the manager was smart to go to his top people - if anyone could pull it off, they could.' And you'd be right! I agree with you that it's probably the best thing to do when <u>in a pinch</u>. However, it should never become the new norm. The bailout syndrome is when this kind of behavior becomes a habit. Month after month, goal after goal, the sales manager finds himself in the same position just a few days before the month-end. Again, and again he runs to his top performers to pull off the miracle. The point here is the sales manager's attention should have been on the newer and underperforming salespeople all along.

If the sales manager were a leader, (utilizing Mentorship), the number one priority would have been to make sure those who need the most guidance, support, and training get it! The focus should be on ensuring every member of the team, especially the least skilled, is receiving all the support and tools they need to be successful. This approach in time will ward off those last-minute month-end situations, preventing the bailout syndrome.

Secondly, the bailout syndrome can have a negative effect on your top performers. If your senior people hit their goal every month, if your best performers are always completing projects on time, that's great! Keep it that way. The worst thing you can do is keep going to them and raising the bar or asking for more to make up for others' shortcomings. I'm sure many of you have seen this firsthand. The result is your top performers can soon get burnout and either stop performing as well as they used to, or in most cases, they find employment elsewhere. The goals set become meaningless to them because they know if they hit their target, you'll just ask for more.

Even worse, I've seen multiple cases where the bailout syndrome is elevated, pertaining to how one manages a team. For example, when the number one salesperson, who used to enjoy flexible working hours because of his/her high performance, is now forced to a strict standard work schedule. This happens when a manager idiotically thinks to himself, "If someone can sell as much as they do in 30 hours a week, imagine what they can sell in 50 hours?" What they mean is, "if he/she can sell, even more, it will make my job a lot easier, and I'll look even better!" Unfortunately, that's not the logic that emanates from genuine leadership, nor is it the thoughts of a real mentor.

Becoming a Confidante

If the lifeblood or foundation of a true leader is Mentorship, then that Mentorship should carry far beyond your direct reports. In other words, leaders are mentors 24/7, and not just when it relates to their subordinates or specific job function.

In my last book, The Executive Arena, we discussed the importance of selecting and using a confidante and utilizing the "transfer of Knowledge" that comes from developing such relationships. I wrote: "A confidant can take many forms, be it an executive coach that one pays for, or a best friend you run ideas past from time to time. There are many definitions depending on the source, so, for the sake of argument, let's take a look at The Executive Arena definition: A confidant is a person who is or possibly was a colleague, from whom you can seek advice with certain problems, or solutions to problems, in complete confidence, without the fear of judgment or reprisal. As the word confidante denotes, it's someone you can <u>confide</u> in, and who in turn, can give you sound advice." Does that not have the word "Mentorship" written all over it?

You see, throughout your career, especially early in your climb to success, it is vital you continue to utilize this fantastic support tool called a confidante. However, as you reach higher levels of management on your path to becoming a success, real leaders want to pay it forward. Again, as I've said before, "great leaders don't try to be heroes; they strive to create them." It's time to share your experiences and the wisdom you've gained from those experiences with others, not just those in your charge. Your goal should also be to expand your Mentorship outside your immediate circle of influence. That's what leaders do!

My wife, a senior executive in human resources, had hired a business consultant to come into one of her previous companies to help mentor and coach the senior management team. Let's call him Randy. He worked very closely with my wife and, over time, they learned about and quickly became extremely impressed with each other's talents and abilities. The project was a huge success, and thus, a robust mentoring relationship was formed. Since then, although both moved on to bigger and better things, they still communicate to this day, sometimes on a monthly basis. Additionally, because of this mentoring relationship, I personally have now formed an alliance with Randy, and we act as each other's mentor from time to time, depending on the topic.

<u>In Closing:</u> Now that we have laid the Keel, and thus ready to build the other compartments to our leadership vessel, I genuinely hope you have seized the importance of Mentorship. To ensure this and solidify its magnitude before moving on to the next chapter, I want to be as sheer and direct as possible. If you sincerely want to be successful in management, if you genuinely want to make a lasting impact at your company or within your team or department, if you're going to one day shine as a great leader, then understand this... It's not about you! You cannot be focused on your reputation or possible future accolades, and expect to inspire, influence, and earn the trust and loyalty of those around you. Like oil and water, they just don't mix.

So, when you walk into your place of business tomorrow, pay special attention to what you can do to help those around you be the best they can be. Chris Hadfield, Astronaut, and former Commander of the International Space Station said it best when he said, "Ultimately, leadership is not about glorious crowning acts. It's about keeping your team focused on a goal and motivated to do their best to achieve it, especially when the stakes are high and the consequences really matter. <u>It is about laying the groundwork for others' success, and then standing back and letting them shine.</u>"

LEADERSHIP LESSONS:

1. Mentorship is the KEEL of your leadership vessel. It is the foundation, and by far the <u>most important</u> element in mastering the art of leadership.
2. Regardless of your current position, title, or even the bullet points in your job description, your number one priority should be to <u>ensure those in your charge are successful</u>, period.
3. Lead now, get promoted later. You don't have to be in a leadership role to be a leader. Ryan, and even Marcus from chapter two both displayed elements of leadership which tuned out to be the catalyst in their promotions.
4. Don't fall victim to the Bailout Syndrome. Focus your mentorship on those who need it the most, not those who make your job easier.
5. Share the experiences and the wisdom you've gained from those experiences with others, in addition to those in your charge. Your goal should always be to expand your mentorship outside your immediate circle of influence.
6. Remember, "It's not about you". Be the guiding light, not the spotlight.

Chapter Four: STUDENTSHIP

"The HULL of your leadership vessel is Growth Mindset"

If mentorship is the Keel of your leadership vessel, if your number one priority as a leader is to ensure those in your charge are successful through constant support and training, then the quest for knowledge or having a growth mindset must be the Hull of your ship. Connected to and stretching out from the Keel, the Hull is the outermost frame and body of the vessel. It's the steel or wooden sides of the ship that encloses the entire structure and causes it to float. It's literally what makes a ship a ship. That Hull as it relates to SHIP-building™, and the second most important element in your leadership vessel, is what we call Studentship.

Studentship, put simply, is the state or condition of being a student. This element of leadership means being a committed lifelong learner, understanding that we should learn something new every day, regardless of the source. Studentship, second only to mentorship, is critical to mastering the art of leadership, and here's why. Firstly, if you ever reach a point where you feel you've learned all you need to know to be successful, then your career is over. Whether you define that success as finally being promoted to Vice President or celebrating the 2nd anniversary of your new sandwich shop, any further growth is stifled. Those who develop this "I've arrived" attitude, are often resistant to change, and not very open to advice or suggestions from their employees or business colleagues. They pay no attention to new or up-and-coming industry developments that could have positive (or negative) impacts within their company because "this is the way we've done it for years." Those who don't practice Studentship can unknowingly hurt themselves, the employees they manage, as well as the businesses that employ them. In Short, they lack a growth mindset.

Secondly, how are you as a leader going to mentor those in your charge, and teach them new things, if you are not continually learning new things yourself? Okay, the question is rhetorical, but I'm going to answer it for you anyway: You can't! You cannot be an effective mentor, and thus be an effective leader, without becoming a lifelong learner. Study anyone who is hugely successful and a great leader, and you will see that all are advocates of personal and professional development. I'm not just talking about those looking to become great leaders, or young aspiring executives hoping to be put in charge one day. True leaders are lifelong learners regardless of their level or position.

While doing my own research on the connection between leadership and the growth mindset, I read an article from ChiefExecutive.net, an excellent website for senior management and those seeking to achieve such levels. The article was entitled 'How to Create an Environment of Lifelong Learning as the Leader.' It was written by Ted Bililies, Ph.D. on January 8, 2019. Ted writes, "Over the past several years, CEOs have begun to embrace the importance of becoming lifelong learners. Gone is the "authority figure" ideal of the past, and with it, the idea that the person at an organization's helm, is a fully formed individual who simply must now take action based on years of stored knowledge. Instead, what more people are realizing, is that the best leaders consider themselves to be in a constant state of growth and development. They never stop learning."

Jim Rohn, a world-renowned and award-winning motivational speaker, and author once said, "Work hard at your job, and you'll make a decent living. Work hard on yourself, and you'll make a fortune!" Jim Rohn was talking about continued personal development and, as incredible as he was, he too was a lifelong learner. So, as you can see, to build the Hull of your leadership vessel, to embrace Studentship, all starts with becoming and teaching others to become lifelong learners. The first step in adopting this growth mindset is Personal Development.

The Personal Development Program (PDP)

As I had mentioned in my last book, "The Executive Arena," being good at your job is only half the battle. The other half, if you are to be genuinely fruitful, rests within you. You learned that you had to become a better observer and communicator. You had to master Corporate Political Intelligence, Perceptional Messaging, and how to maneuver within the executive arena successfully. All these skills were about you improving as a person, a colleague, and now a leader. It's not about you being a good electrician, a banker, an engineer, or even an astronaut. It's about accepting the fact that YOU are responsible for the successes and failures of the people you lead. Those who fully own that responsibility, embrace the element of Studentship.

So, what exactly is personal development? Personal development covers numerous activities that improve self-awareness, develop different talents and potential, enhance the quality of life, and contribute to the realization of dreams and aspirations. In short, it's a life-long process of continued learning that's designed to make you a better person! Most companies will support continuing education relating to one's specific job, for example, annual seminars covering the new employment laws going into effect, or formal sales training for the sales department. Unfortunately, a lot of corporations don't support much that relates to one's personal growth. However, leaders or tomorrow (like you) know the value of continued personal development and the number of leaders who truly understand its impact is growing.

So, let's talk about some of the ways you can implement a Personal Development Program (PDP) both for yourself and within your department or organization.

The Leadership Arena

<u>Leaders are Readers, but only ten pages:</u>

I can't count the number of times I've been told that most people are just too busy to become avid readers, let alone instill some sort of reading program into the ranks of their employees. A lot have tried things like the 'Book of the Month' program or the like, which quickly fizzled after the first book or two. Or, the 'required reading' for every new hire or manager, again quickly becoming a thing of the past, perhaps because of the lack of follow-through, among other reasons. However, there is a tactic that I have learned and taught that has proven auspicious time and time again. I learned it many years ago from a mentor of mine by the name of Jeff Olson. Jeff is a fantastic speaker, teacher, and author of "The Slight Edge," a book that literally changed my life, along with his continual mentoring to me and many others. Here is the concept: <u>Read just ten pages of a good book every day</u>. By good book, I mean something in the self-help / personal development category, much like this book. That's it. Just ten pages a day is all it takes to become an avid reader, and here's why.

ANYONE can find the time to read ten pages in 24 hours. Even a slow reader can read ten pages in ten to fifteen minutes. Hell, keep the book next to the toilet if that's the only quiet time you can find, but read those ten short pages. We all know, this routine after 30 days will become a habit. Now here's the kicker. In one year, you will have read 3650 pages. With the average self-help/personal development book being about 250 pages long, you would have read almost 15 books! Do you think reading 15 books in a year will have an effect on you and your career? Absolutely! Even if the average books you read were a little longer than 250 pages each, and you only read 12 books in a year, that's one book a month which more than qualifies you as an avid reader.

What's really amazing about the 10-pages concept is the fact that it's easily rolled out and accepted, for obvious reasons, throughout a department or organization. Here are some suggested tips to successfully implement the 10-pages concept:

1. <u>Let the employee choose what to read</u>. As long as the book is of the personal or professional development category, let them choose! Of course, it's okay to suggest or even have a list of recommended reading to choose from but, the point here is you are giving them the freedom to choose what they feel will be the most beneficial to them. You are also conveying that you trust in their decision.
2. <u>Implement break-time for self-improvement</u>. Look, let's face it – all employees take numerous breaks throughout the day, whether official or not. Be it a smoke break, a round of Solitaire on their laptop, a walk outside to get some fresh air, or logging on to grab a quick update from their favorite social media page. It's happening all around us, so trying to police this inevitable paradigm is futile. Instead,

let's take advantage of this already formed habit and instill Studentship in the workplace! Officially announce that everyone is allowed 15 – 30 minutes each day for self-Improvement. IE: reading their ten pages, watching a YouTube video on leadership, or researching a possible seminar they may want to attend, (discussed later). This time should be in addition to, not in place of one's lunch break or other allotted breaks.

3. <u>Official follow-up Routines.</u> Once this program is implemented, it is crucial for its longevity to have formal follow-up routines. As a leader of Studentship, you will want to get regular updates on your people's personal development. If you are currently in a leadership position, you are most likely already having one-on-one meetings, be it weekly, bi-weekly, or monthly with your staff. (If you're not, I highly suggest you start). During these meetings, after you knock out the regular work-related updates and discussions, end the session on a high note with a follow-up on their self-improvement regimen. How do they like the book so far? What chapter are they on? What have they learned? Would they recommend the book to others? Additionally, is there is a seminar someone on your team wants to attend or an excellent 20-minute video someone found on YouTube, that others on the team would benefit from viewing?

In short, however you decide to manage a Personal Development Plan, having formal follow-up routines sends a clear message that personal and professional development is highly valued in your department or organization. Additionally, Self-Improvement, as a graded category, can easily be added to the employee's annual review, breathing new life into an ancient, stressful, and sometimes outdated process.

Drive-Time University:

You may have heard that the first audiobook was released in the early 1950s, while others say it was even further back in the 1940s, but that's just not true. The audiobook, believe it or not, first emerged back in 1932 (yes, you read that correctly), by the American Foundation for the Blind. By creating their own recording studio, and recording narrators reading different types of text, books became available on vinyl records, much like your favorite music was sold. As technology advanced, along came audiobooks on the cassette tape in the 1960s followed by books on CD or Compact Disc in the 1980s. With a reputation initially labeled as a medium for "people who don't like to read" or the "Lazy way to read," listening to audiobooks today has quickly become highly accepted and extremely popular. I personally partake in this technology and actually advocate its extensive usage. With [Audible](www.audible.com) being the top, and in my opinion, the best audiobook platform available, I utilize and promote what I like to call, Drive-Time University (DTU), or Drive-time YOU.

Whether you are the frequently traveling woman executive, or the ever-growing stay-at-home-dad (SAHD), we all spend a considerable amount of time commuting. From rush hour traffic dropping kids at school to business flights and long security lines at the airport, this downtime can be transformed into good times! The average American spends over an hour per day behind the wheel, with a good percentage doubling and even tripling that statistic. But instead of just listening to music, or (God forbid) the bombarding streams of negativity and loathing we call "News," why not put that time to good use? If you're one of those busy people that can't seem to find the time to read, then Drive-Time University is the solution. So, download the Audible app, pick a book that interests you, and turn that hour per day into the most valuable time there is – YOU TIME!

Shadowing:

One of the most effective tools I have ever used pertaining to Studentship is Shadowing. I'm sure we can all agree that, regardless of the organization you may be working for, there is always a certain amount of animosity, department bashing, or "finger-pointing" that goes on between departments. "Accounting did this," or "we can't finish the project because purchasing is dragging their feet." I remember a specific situation while working for a retail giant as their Regional Director. While selling computers and electronics was the company's bread and butter, they also sold computer training to corporations. It was sold as sort of an add-on benefit. When a company would come in and purchase, let's say 175 computers, the salesperson would offer exclusive deals on training for their staff. Once the sales department closed the deal, it was then the responsibility of the training department to deliver the promised training. Anyway, the assigned Instructor physically bring laptop computers to the client's site to deliver whatever training was agreed upon. Once training was performed, the salesperson got a phone call from the client complaining about the training. "Hey," the client said, "I remember you telling me the Instructor would teach Microsoft Outlook, that he would spend about an hour going over the basics of using email? Well, that never happened!" The salesperson, now upset, goes to his boss and complains that the instructor "messed things up," and the blame game begins.

Clearly, there was some level of miscommunication that prompted this phone call, however, where that took place, or what actually happened is not relevant to this lesson. What is important is that these types of situations between departments exist on many levels and in many organizations. The sales department blames the service department for not providing an excellent service. The service department blames the sales department for "overselling" the service or promising extra stuff to "land the deal." This type of finger-pointing is common and can truly take a toll on a company's culture, and most times, these fires are made worse by the department managers themselves.

The Leadership Arena

In this particular instance, we implemented Shadowing. Firstly, the sales manager was ordered to shadow the training manager for an entire day. Not just for a couple of hours, or pop in a couple of meetings; he had to shadow him for the whole day, literally. Once that was complete, the training manager had to do the same with the sales manager. Additionally, throughout the next 30-days or so, the Salespeople and Instructors (one at a time, of course, as to not hinder overall business operations) had to shadow their counterparts as well. The Instructor actually had to listen to the salesperson make sales calls, negotiate pricing with clients, etc., and the salespeople went out onsite with the Instructor to observe them dealing with and delivering training to clients. It's a very effective tool because, as with most of these situations, its more a lack of misunderstanding than it is miscommunication.

You see, by employing this element of Studentship, employees develop a mutual understanding of each other's job, and the challenges each one faces in a typical day. Furthermore, a solid bridge of mutual respect is built, which opens the door for improved lines of communication between departments. Moreover, it's a great way to foster an "Ownership" mentality (discussed later) within the ranks, because they see "the big picture" when it comes to overall company operations. It should be noted here that not every employee in a department needs to be involved in shadowing. In the situation mentioned above, I felt it was warranted, but in most cases, It's not. The department managers' involvement, having the influence they do, is sufficient since they set the tone for their department in most cases.

Lastly, the use of shadowing is a beautiful tool to simply promote Studentship and continued life-long learning. There doesn't need to be an "issue" or problem between departments before this fantastic tool can be put into action. In summary, mutual respect, understanding other vital roles, and cross-training is what makes the members of a military special forces' unit so effective, and it works in a corporate environment as well.

Investment in Studentship Builds Loyalty

"Employees who believe that management is concerned about them as a whole person - not just an employee - are more productive, more satisfied, more fulfilled. Satisfied employees mean satisfied customers, which leads to profitability." - Anne M. Mulcahy.

I am a firm believer that if you don't invest in your people, especially your best employees, someone else surely will. I'm not talking about purchasing business cards, office supplies, or a mini-fridge for the office (though the mini-fridge would earn you some pretty cool brownie points). Nor do I mean paying for the CPE course your accountant needs to take each year to keep his/her CPA certification. Those are not investments per se; those are tools necessary to do the job, that you should be providing regardless. I'm talking about genuinely investing in things that will make your employees better, more well-rounded people overall. Because when you invest in the personal development of your people, you are illustrating that you care about them as a whole person, not just an employee. When you do this correctly, you set yourself apart from the average manager or employer, and that my friend builds loyalty!

Loyalty is by far one of the most critical traits you should strive to achieve from your people. You can teach someone a skill, you can teach someone about leadership, but you can't teach someone to be loyal. That comes from within, and only after the employee truly believes you care about them.

Let's discuss some investments in Studentship that will pay dividends when it comes to personal development, and thus build loyalty in those that matter most.

Retreats and Consultants:

Another useful tool when investing in Studentship is really a combination of utilizing both retreats and consultants. By retreats, I mean any event that's at least one full day in length that takes place outside of the office, anywhere except your place of business. Many years ago, while working for a tech company, I hired a fantastic sales trainer we will call Michael. I hired him to do a two-day session at the annual management retreat we were holding in Las Vegas. I had all the GMs fly in for four days to provide them some robust sales and leadership training, as well as provide a casual setting to share best practices from around the country. I had recently been promoted to vice president and, with the actual president, CEO, and both founders of the company in attendance, this had to go off well for my career's sake, if you know what I mean. I had known Michael for many years as I had been through many of his sales/leadership training sessions at a previous company. His message and teaching style really hit home with me, and I became a raving fan of his teachings very early in my career. I continue to teach his lessons to this day. The point here is this: I could have easily been the one to teach this 2-day training session. Additionally, I could have held the training at our company headquarters, or even via a webinar, so no one had to travel. But would the training have been as effective? Even if I were just as great a presenter (which I'm wasn't) and the material I presented was the exact information Michael taught, would it have had the same impact?

The answer is a resounding no and for a couple reasons.

Firstly, having a company function off-site comes with many positive benefits:

1. <u>It Limits Distractions:</u> By removing the employees from their working environment, you are eliminating or limiting the daily disruptions that go along with it. Your team will be more able to focus on the subject matter at hand, versus worrying about day to day tasks.

2. <u>It Inspires Creativity:</u> It's a fact that when people are at work, they are in "work mode," and with that comes a certain professional way to carry yourself. For the most part, we watch what we say, and we go about our day with a deliberate professional persona. However, remove the familiar working environment, and people let their guard down. They open up and believe it or not, become more openminded. These different surroundings inspire creativity and out-of-box thinking!
3. <u>It Strengthens Teamwork:</u> With more time to get to know each other (outside of work), team members begin to realize what makes the other person tick? They learn each other's likes and dislikes, and real personalities start to surface. Toss in a glass of wine or favorite cocktail, and you can almost see the cohesive magic that bonds your team getting stronger.

Secondly, hiring a consultant or outside speaker/presenter brings even more significant benefits to your already positive off-site atmosphere:

1. <u>It Builds Acceptance:</u> Using the example discussed previously, if you bring in your GM's to learn something new, in the hopes it will be rolled out in their perspective locations upon their return, they must believe in what they've heard. You can tell your employees "dress for success", for example, until you're blue in the face, and it will never have

the same level of impact, compared to those same words spoken by someone outside the company. As strange as it seems, lessons being taught by an "expert" you brought in carries much more weight than having, let's say the training department deliver the same material. Employee acceptance of lessons or topics being presented is vital; without it, the subsequent "take action" steps will never happen.

2. <u>It Fosters Loyalty:</u> When you hire an outside consultant, speaker, trainer, whatever don't think for a second that it goes unnoticed. What I mean is, your employees know darn well that the person doing the presenting isn't doing it for free. They know you had to pay them, and I guarantee, in most cases, they will assume the fee is much higher than actually paid. The point here is, this builds loyalty because they realize you are investing in their development. They will appreciate the fact that you or the company is spending hard-earned money on helping them become a better leader, a better salesman, or overall a better person... and that builds loyalty.

3. <u>It Brings New Perspectives:</u> When listening to a speaker or trainer present material, what may hit home for one person, may have absolutely no effect on another. This is because everyone learns in different ways. After all, our brains are unique, and we are all wired differently. If you study many

of the top motivational speakers in the world today, you will quickly notice that they all are teaching the same life-lessons, or "secrets," they are just presenting them in different ways. These different approaches to the same lesson is a good thing because, while you may have been killing yourself trying to motivate your team by presenting an experience or sales tactic you thought was terrific, an outsider may get the job done by presenting differently. More importantly, new perspectives spawn new ideas and innovation, an invaluable asset to any leader.

In summary, never underestimate the power of retreats and consultants. Even if only on a small scale, like inviting your 4-person team to your home on a Saturday, to discuss goals for the next quarter, the impact can be immeasurable. While the return on investment may sometimes be hard to track, the long-term effect does pay dividends in the form of loyalty, creativity, and teamwork. And that my friend is invaluable in the leadership arena.

Memberships and Seminars:

While this next section should be a no-brainer, I am still surprised how many organizations don't utilize this easy and generally inexpensive form of Studentship. In today's competitive world, job seekers consider much more than salary when looking for that next employment opportunity.

They also look at the benefits, but I'm not talking about the standard medical and dental benefits related to healthcare. I'm talking about everything else, the extra stuff that most employers don't even consider, let alone list in their job descriptions. Things like the ability to work from home when the appliance repair guy is on his way to fix your fridge, or the daughter is sick, and daycare won't accept any child with a fever. Or, as is the subject of this section, the benefit of having job-related memberships or seminars paid for by the employer.

There is a plethora of membership opportunities and seminars related to just about every profession and position. The Society of Human Resource Management or SHRM, for short, is a must membership for anyone in the HR department. There are local chapters, state-wide and national chapters depending on your budget. The National Society of Accountants or NSA is another membership opportunity, obviously for people in your accounting department. Then there is the occasional seminar or training course, including topics ranging from leadership to project management, from effective communication to strategic planning.

This wide array of learning opportunities is just one more way of promoting Studentship within your organization. Continued learning promotes, and fuels continued growth, which, in turn, brings profitability. I'm not saying you

The Leadership Arena

have to pay for everything, as each employee should take responsibility for their own continued learning. However, providing a professional monthly membership or covering the cost of the occasional "vital skill" improving seminar, quite simply, proves that your organization values Studentship, and is leading that charge by example.

Field Trips:

We all remember the field trips we took in school as a child. The oh so popular tour to the science museum, or the observatory was widespread. The all-day trip to the local zoo or amusement park, I'm sure we can all agree were among the most memorable. We took these field trips in our early years for many reasons, including but not limited to, enhancing our understanding of specific topics as well as to improve cultural experiences. It was a way to get out of the classroom, build strong relationships while learning something valuable in the process. But, then along came graduation, and unfortunately, the term "field trip" became defined as a childhood event, quickly becoming an adolescent memory.

But it doesn't have to be that way! For the very same reason field trips were so useful in our early development, leaders of tomorrow are bringing back these "Learning Expeditions" in today's corporate arena. Additionally, these trips or expeditions do not have to be directly related to one's industry or a specific area of development. What I mean is, a journey for your creative design department doesn't have to be to some prestigious art museum. As an example, remember the sales and training departments we discussed earlier? Perhaps a combined trip to the local zoo would help strengthen the bond between departments. Just remember the actual act of taking one of these trips, is just as crucial, if not more, as where you go. If you can combine an educational benefit with the excursion, then all the better, but remember, Studentship is about growth in all areas of life, not just job-related.

Before I bring this chapter to a close, I have to share with you a memory I have that is still as vivid today as it was the day it happened. As Michael (mentioned previously) went about his presentation to the GM's, Kevin, the president of the company, was sitting next to me at the back of the class. As we were both smiling, equally enjoying Michael's unique delivery style, Kevin leaned over towards me and said: "Great job on hiring this guy… you deserve the kudos."

The point here once again is to promote Studentship! To advocate for continued life-long learning both for yourself, but more importantly, for those in your charge. Furthermore, that learned knowledge or skill gained doesn't have to come directly from you. So, hire the consultant, bring in the speaker, and plan that retreat or learning expedition. Because being in a constant state of Studentship, helping those around you to grow and be successful, will ultimately bring success back to you.

LEADERSHIP LESSONS:

The Leadership Arena

1. Built upon and extending out from the Keel is what is called the Hull. That Hull as it relates to SHIP-building™, and the second most important element in your leadership vessel, is what we call Studentship.
2. Studentship is being in a constant state of life-long learning. As Jim Rohn once said, "Work hard at your job and you'll make a decent living. Work hard on yourself and you'll make a fortune!"
3. Those who don't practice studentship can unknowingly hurt themselves, the employees they manage, as well as the businesses that employ them.
4. Leaders of tomorrow know the real value of continued personal development. Through Personal Development Programs (PDP's) you can enhance the continued learning and growth of the whole person not just the employee aspect.
5. You can teach someone a skill, you can teach someone about leadership, but you can't teach someone how to be loyal. However, utilizing PDP elements like Drive-Time University, Shadowing and reading 10-pages a day; instills Studentship, and thus builds loyalty in those you lead.
6. Never underestimate the power of retreats and consultants. Even if only on a small scale, like inviting your 4-person team to your home on a Saturday, or a Lunch-n-Learn about effective communication, the impact is literally immeasurable!

Chapter Five: DIRECTORSHIP

The Necessary and Most Difficult Part of Being the Boss!

The Boatswain's Whistle sounded the beginning of another ordinary Navy working day in port. Or though we thought. The sound of this irritating whistle was almost ear piercing, consisting of multiple sliding tones used to differentiate between types of calls or announcements. In this case, the noise we heard was followed by the words, "All hands report to your duty stations for Muster, Instruction, and Inspection." In other words, it was kind of like taking attendance at the beginning of each day. We would all gather (Muster) to ensure everyone was present, discuss any specific things we needed to get done that day (Instruction), and, lastly, of course, make sure everyone was appropriately dressed and looked like they were supposed to look, (Inspection). You know, clean-shaven, clean uniforms, etc.

On this day, we were dressed in what the Navy called Dungarees. Dungarees, back in the 1980s, was the working uniform for sailors, which frankly looked like prison uniforms from the 1940s. The Dungarees consisted of flared or "bell bottom" blue jeans, worn with a short-

The Leadership Arena

sleeved or long-sleeved denim-colored blue collared shirt. Aside from the hat we wore, the only distinction between prisoners' garb and the Navy working uniform was the fact that we had our last name stenciled above the right pocket. Change that last name to a serial number, and rest assured you'd get some strange looks out in town. It's my guess this is why we were not allowed to wear dungarees outside of the naval base. It's either that or they lacked the impressiveness of the widely popular dress blues or dress white uniforms called Cracker Jacks. Regardless of how many of us complained about the uniform, the dungarees were very practical. They were sturdy, durable, easy to clean, and frankly lasted for what seemed like forever.

Since my shipmates and I worked in engineering, we would generally start our days in the engine room, which on an aircraft carrier was located many decks (floors) below the waterline. However, today was different as we were instructed to muster on the flight deck. This usually meant something special was going on. Perhaps the Captain was going to address the crew, or someone was getting promoted, or some other "outside the ordinary" reason. Whatever the case, it was a refreshing change to be outside, soaking up some Florida morning sun. Even in March, it was already 78 degrees at 0700 hours (7 AM).

"Here he comes," Erikson announced, "Let's do this!" We all looked over to take note of Petty Officer Casper heading our way from across the flight deck and snapped to attention. Casper was our POIC or Petty Officer in Charge. He was a First-Class Petty officer (E-6) and in charge of our engine room. Casper was a great guy and very dedicated to the Navy. He was a short but stocky guy, slightly balding and earned the nickname Danny DeVito, from the TV series Taxi because of the way he used to yell at people from inside the supply cage. He was what sailors called a "lifer" defined as someone who would most likely stay in the Navy until retirement (20 years of service) or perhaps even longer. Some lifers have been known to serve for up to 30 years or more, which is considered extremely honorable.

As Casper approach our formation, Erikson took one step forward and announced, "Good morning Petty Officer, all present or accounted for." Casper nodded his head and replied, "Very well... At Ease, everyone". The command At Ease meant we could just casually stand there, in no particular stance. In other words, just relax. "Listen up, everyone, I have a bit of bad news," Casper began. "As you know, we are three weeks away from Sea Trials. This upcoming evolution will be filled with back to back military drills and inspections every day for the entire 30 days at sea. We must pass sea trials with flying colors, or all our hard work will be for not." I took a deep breath and could feel the tension in my muscles increase as I braced for the bad news. Casper continued. "While I know this division has worked extremely hard readying ourselves, there are other divisions on this ship that are still lacking in performance, and they need our help. So, starting tomorrow, the Captain has ordered working hours for the entire ship to be extended to 16 hours per day for the remainder of our time in port." Casper barely got out the last three words of 'time in port' before the grunts, moans, and verbal complaints began.

As I closed my eyes in disbelief, my ears were filled with a plethora of colorful metaphors ringing out all around me. You know, such popular phrases like 'That's bullshit,' and 'you've got to be fucking kidding me' were only a few of the less-offensive sailor-type jargon that rang out. As I opened my eyes and took another deep breath, accepting the news I had just heard, I noticed Casper getting frustrated as the redness in his cheeks grew darker. "Attention!" Casper ordered loudly, dragging out the "E" in the word attention. We all snapped to attention, realizing at the same time that we just crossed the line with Casper. "Let me tell you all something right now," Casper ordered loudly. "You are a Sailor in the United States Navy, not some shelf-stocking Walmart employee that can call in sick anytime they want because of the sniffles." His voice raised, "Our captain has asked for our help, and that's exactly what we are going to do, so SUCK IT UP!" We all stood in silence. Casper dropped his head and looked down at the deck as if he were searching for the next proper thing to say. "Look," he began in a much lower but still firm tone. "These new hours don't go into effect until tomorrow. So, today when you go home, hug the wife, kiss the kids, take the family out to dinner, hell get drunk for all I care, and blow off steam, but be back here tomorrow morning ready to do your job. Understand?" Besides being a rhetorical question, no one dared respond while standing at attention. Casper turned and left the formation giving his final command, "Dismissed."

As Casper headed off below decks, Erikson jokingly spirted out, "There's no way he's actually married, is there?" We all chuckled. "Rumor has it, his family has to salute him when he walks in a room," another injected. We continued to joke, laugh, and smile. Deep inside, we all respected Casper, but regardless, the jokes and bashing continued as we all dispersed across the flight deck.

I was the Administrative Petty officer and had some work to do before reporting to the engine room, so I headed to our Admin office. As I headed down the last ladder (stairwell) by the admin office, I could hear what sounded like Casper cursing and swearing. When I reach the office, the door was open, so of course, I walked in. Casper was on the phone, his back initially towards me, but as I walked in further, he could see me through his peripheral vision. I walked over and took a seat behind the admin desk, and began my work. Casper continued what became clear was a conversation with his wife. "This is a bunch of bullshit, I know. My guys worked their asses off, and for what? To get screwed! Because we outperformed other divisions, we get rewarded with extended hours and more hard work. I'm so pissed right now." There was a short pause before the call ended with a much softer, "Okay, babe, I'll see you tonight. I love you". Casper hung up the phone, and with his back still facing me, put his hands on his hips, took a deep breath, and stood there for a few seconds.

I was so amazed by the conversation I had just heard; I had to state the obvious. "So, you feel the same way we all do about the extended hours?" I questioned in a matter-of-fact tone. As Casper began to walk towards the office door, he turned his head to look over his shoulder in my direction. With a wink and slight smile, no doubt acknowledging the correctness of my statement, Casper left the office without saying a word. It was at that moment; that exact point in time, I began to learn what Directorship was all about.

Never Bite the Hand That Feeds You

I can't tell you how many times I have witnessed people bad-mouthing the company they work for, or the person or persons they have to work with, or both. I've made these obvious observations both in person at networking functions and other face-to-face events, as well as on numerous social media platforms. I'm amazed at the sheer number of times I've seen this kind of unprofessional and sometimes even disrespectful behavior. With that, I should also share another blatantly obvious observation. Almost every time I've witnessed this behavior, it never came from those in positions of leadership. To put it more clearly, you will never see a VP of Finance at a major bank, or the Director of Marketing for a law firm, partaking in this kind of immature ranting. This connection is not coincidental. It's because real leaders understand a fundamental rule when it comes to Directorship: <u>Never Bite the Hand That Feeds You</u>!

Richard Spector

Most people assume that when you are promoted into a management position, an increase in salary is accompanied by an increase in your day to day responsibilities. However, it doesn't stop there. There are three essential points to remember pertaining to this "don't bite" rule. Let's review them now.

1. <u>Support the Company Mission, Vision and Direction</u>: When you are hired for a leadership position, or finally promoted into one, you must fully accept that what is expected of you, stretches well beyond your job description. In the Leadership Arena, you need to understand that being granted a position of leadership means that you are now becoming an extension of the company. Whether on-the-clock or outside of work, you become an ambassador of that company or company's brand. In addition to the bullet points listed in your job description, your job is always to support the company's mission, vision, and direction. This support includes those times when you don't agree with a company's decision or the sudden organizational change in the way it operates. Look, I'm not saying you must agree 100% with every decision the company or your superiors make, but as a leader, you MUST support and "act in accordance with" supporting those decisions.

Let's go back to the previous story about Casper, who was my supervisor earlier in my naval career.

When he told the department about the extended working hours, of course, he too was upset about the decision. But he didn't show it, at least not to a public audience. He was not going to let his personal feelings disrupt the team's positive momentum or allow us to become disengaged from the mission at hand. Casper's ability to direct, motivate, and inspire his team going forward would have compromised if Casper had come into that meeting, bitching and complaining right along with the other team members. Instead, he stood firm when he noticed his team's morale beginning to slide, keeping them focused on the task at hand, then later venting his frustrations to his wife. The point is, there is always a time and place to "become one of the guys," but this was NOT one of those situations.

2. <u>Respect the Chain-of-Command</u>: This is by far one of the most enforced leadership rules in the military. It pertains to respecting one's rank and position and is extremely important in a military environment. However, this rule should also transfer over to the corporate environment as equally important. Simply put, to respect the chain-of-command means you <u>don't go over anyone's head</u>. You don't go around or bypass your immediate supervisor for any reason, regardless of your level or position. Even if you don't like the orders you were given, or because you think it would just be quicker to do so, you always respect

the chain-of-command. For example, let's say you felt you deserved a raise because of all the hard work you've been doing as of late. You've been given more responsibility, and thus, you think it's time to present your case for a salary increase. The worst thing you can do is to go above your boss's head (to your boss's boss), or directly to the person you think has the highest chance of saying "yes." Doing so is not only unprofessional, but you are sending perceptional messages to your boss that could be interpreted as 'you don't respect him or her', or 'you feel that their opinion doesn't matter.' Going this route will almost inevitably result in your request being denied, not to mention damage to any positive relationship you may have had with your immediate supervisor. Instead, by following the chain-of-command and going to your boss first, you may enlist the help of your boss to be your cheerleader. It is they, who can then become your advocate presenting your case to the powers that be. Trust me, your boss declaring you need a raise carries much more weight than those words coming from you.

Critical Note: There is only one reason you can and should go over your boss's head. In the case of illegal or unethical activity, such as sexual harassment or racial bias, for example, it is not only your right; it is your responsibility to report it. In those situations, you should

> go to the person's direct supervisor or Human Resources, whichever you feel most comfortable.

3. <u>Always Honor your Values and Ethics</u>: "Winning is nice if you don't lose your integrity in the process!" -Arnold Horshack, a character on "Welcome Back Kotter" (1975-1979) TV Series.

   There will most surely come a time in your career where your values or ethics, just don't match your employer's direction or the way they operate. Perhaps you are customer-service driven, but your employer's mission, vision, and value statements are all focused on "satisfying our stockholders" and selling, selling, selling. Or perhaps you've witnessed things that are unethical or even borderline illegal, and you are just not comfortable working within that kind of culture. Even in those situations, a great leader will not degrade or otherwise bad-mouth the company to anyone, as we discussed in the first point. However, that doesn't mean you just swallow your pride and live with it. As a real leader, working within the realm of Directorship, you should continue to support the company's mission, vision and direction, (in other words, do your job) until you find employment elsewhere. Yes, you read that correctly. The fantastic position you have, the great pay and benefits, the company car, the free tickets to see your favorite professional sports teams, are all great! Nevertheless, as enjoyable as these benefits can be, you should never have to sacrifice your values and ethics to get them. Doing so only weakens your character and can hinder your continued growth as a leader. It's best just to move on.

Critical Note: Your leadership style and ultimately your success as a leader, will be forged in large part, by the values and ethics you hold dear.

Nepotism – It's All About Perception

I had initially struggled with where in the book to include this next section. As a leader or future leader, you may be in a position of power and influence over setting company policies or standards that will ultimately affect company culture. I could have easily fit this topic just about anywhere, but nepotism, being an issue that births its pretty head during the hiring phase, I thought it best be discussed here in the "being the Boss" or Directorship chapter.

I have had many teaching discussions around the topic of nepotism and have done extensive research on whether it's a good practice or not in the workplace. I have heard some very valid arguments from both sides of the coin and have witnessed firsthand some situations that have worked out wonderfully. Additionally, people have stated to me things like, "My brother and I work great together" and "even though he's my nephew, I don't cut him any slack." or "my sister works over in purchasing... I do not affect her career as the Director of Sales". I've also heard some real genuine statements like "I don't base my hiring decisions on whether someone is family or not... they better be able to do the job". While all these stated situations are valid arguments, the real problem with nepotism is seldomly realized. Its kind of like all these arguments are merely addressing the symptoms and not the disease.

The real problem with nepotism is not about the brother, the sister, or the wife related to someone else at the company. I'm sure we can all agree that hiring someone based purely on the fact that they are family is wrong. All hiring decisions should be based on one's qualifications and ability to do the job successfully. It should never be based on race, gender, age, or any of the wonderful "protected classes" the government has carved into law, and rightly so. The problem with nepotism, however, doesn't rest with whether the person is qualified. Even if you were able to ignore the fact that a potential candidate was related to someone else in the company, it doesn't matter. If the candidate was the most qualified and the best fit for the job, <u>it doesn't matter</u>. You see, it's not the candidate that's the problem, it's the perceptions of everyone else. The real damaging effects of nepotism are its effect on everyone BUT the family members involved!

You see, regardless of how you justify it or explain it to employees, they will always think favoritism was somehow involved. For example, let's say this person is promoted or awarded Employee of the Month. The fact that they are related to someone else of influence will always be a question in the minds of others. Feelings like this are unavoidable and will continuously come up affecting morale, company culture, and can lead to animosity, producing an atmosphere not conducive to growth and success. Furthermore, it's not fair to the recipient of nepotism, either. Do you think it's fair to that person when people begin to say, "Be careful what you say around Bill, he's the boss's nephew." Or, "Joanne only got that award because she's the president's daughter." Whichever side of the argument you may sit, one fact is indisputable. Nepotism brings sometimes-undetected feelings of jealousy, resentment, and overall bad blood, neither of which contributes to effective leadership or teamwork.

In my professional opinion, nepotism is never a good idea in any organization that genuinely strives for a culture of solidarity. As leaders, I believe we have a responsibility to educate others on the real effects this can have, and why such rules against nepotism should be more commonplace whenever possible.

The Most Difficult Conversations – Dealing with Problem Employees

The Leadership Arena

When it comes to mastering the art of leadership through SHIP-building™ this next section in the area of "being the boss" or Directorship, is by far the most difficult to master for most genuine leaders. In fact, it is the single most challenging element of Directorship one must overcome, and a challenge many leaders struggle with over and over again. I'm talking about dealing with problem employees. It's those difficult conversations that we all know must take place from time to time, but we hate to have them, nonetheless. It's very uncomfortable, I know it is, and I'll be the first to admit it.

I have had to discipline and fire many people throughout my career, and I'm here to tell you, I don't care how many times you've had to do it, it never gets easier. That said, let me assure you of this: It's uncomfortable because <u>you care</u>! It's challenging and unpleasant because you genuinely care about your people and their success. As we have already discussed, leaders are mentors, and as you go about your day coaching and mentoring your people towards success, it's hard to have to turn around now and slap their hand, or worse yet, terminate someone because they made a mistake. So yes, it's awkward, and it is uncomfortable, and it will never get any easier.

Now, on the other end of the spectrum is the manager that feels his/her first line of defense is to write someone up or terminate them as a way to control their people. We talked about this type of person in my last book, The Executive Arena. The Trigger Finger, as I call them, is the exact opposite of a mentor. They don't understand the difference between leadership and management. The trigger finger believes it's a lot easier just to fire someone and start over, rather than coaching and training someone to succeed. These are the managers who sometimes use a "cattle call" hiring method, for example, something I've personally witnessed firsthand. A cattle-call is where managers quickly hire a bunch of people through group-type interviews, then with little to no training, just toss them into the job and to see who sticks. It's a process that appears to work on the surface but at significant cost to the company because of extremely high turnover, not to mention the human aspect and unethical cultures it creates. In short, those who implement the trigger finger mentality are not leaders. So, if you find yourself developing a pit at the bottom of your stomach because you need to have that uncomfortable conversation with a member of your team, you're in good company.

Look, I know, as real leaders, we want our entire team and organization to succeed! Having a reliable team of hard-working, dedicated, and continuously motivated employees are excellent! It's what every leader wants, and we continually strive to make that happen. When all pistons are firing, and the leadership engine is running correctly, great things happen, and it's undoubtedly a beautiful thing to experience. Unfortunately, reality sets in, and the famous phrase "shit happens" seems to find a way to sneak back into our lives and remind us that Murphy (the bastard that created his own law) is still alive and doing quite well.

The Leadership Arena

Throughout your career, there will always be situations where you, as a leader, must step in, confront, address, or otherwise deal with problem employees or situations. These issues can vary from something as simple as chronic tardiness to more complex issues like poor marketing results from your Director of Advertising.

Whatever the issue, there comes a time where that dreaded "difficult conversation" must take place. Whether it's a first offense or the third and final warning before termination, it's never a situation one looks forward to performing.

I don't care how seasoned of an executive you may be; it still sucks to be the "bad guy" and discipline a member of your team. To make matters worse, I've known of situations where a specific employee was a fantastic worker but had attendance issues. They were one of the best performers on the entire team; that is when they showed up for work.

I'll be the first to admit that when you have a poor performer who suddenly develops attendance issues or some other work jeopardizing problem on top of it, psychologically, it does make it a lot easier to deal with the situation—hey, just being honest. But when you have a top-notch performer, well-liked and respected by all, who begins to take a turn for the worse, the term "difficult conversation" reaches a whole new level. It's like you almost have to fight the urge to forgive or turn the other cheek because they are such a valued member of the team. You may even begin to doubt your decision to have the conversation at all, and wondering will sitting them down and having that heart-to-heart only make matters worse? It can be tough, but again that feeling is reasonable because you care.

As a good manager and leader, you know having that counseling session is crucial if you value that particular member of your team. So how, as a leader, do you have this conversation? What is the most effective way to correct someone's challenges or shortcomings, while at the same time ensuring them, they are still a valued member of the team? In the Navy, considering the reputation sailors have for colorful metaphors, we called it the Shit Sandwich. However, many years later and after significant maturing, I now call it the PCT Method or quite simply, The Sandwich.

The PCT Method – "The Sandwich"

Michael walked into the director's office, placed his cell phone on the conference table as he took a seat at the far end near the large office windows overlooking the city. It was a fantastic view from the 14th floor, and that seat would give Michael something to look at while he waited for his boss to arrive. As Michael looked down at the tiny slow-moving cars and ant-sized people shuffling through the morning rush-hour-filled streets, he could feel drops of sweat begin to run from his armpits. Nervous about why he was called to Craig's office, Michael took a couple of slow deep breaths in an attempt to calm himself. It wasn't working. He had somewhat of an idea

The Leadership Arena

as to why this meeting was called and was preparing for the worst. He knew his sales team hadn't been performing as of late, and 'maybe today' (Michael thought to himself), was the day he was getting fired. "Whatever happens, happens," Michael mumbled out loud, trying to convince himself that everything would be okay, and whatever happens is probably for the better. That wasn't working either.

The office door opened, and Craig stepped into his office while in mid-conversation. "Thanks, Janet," he said to his assistant, who sat just outside the office entrance, "I'll take care of it this afternoon." Craig shut the door with a smile and noticed Michael sitting at the end of the conference table. Michael began to stand up but was interrupted. "No, please, sit, Michael." Craig insisted. "I'll come over to you, just let me grab my stuff." He sat back down, while Craig grabbed a folder and writing pad off his desk and walked over to where Michael was sitting. "It doesn't matter how many times I walk in this office; the view never gets old," Craig said as he pulled out a chair and took a seat directly across the table from Michael. "It's pretty amazing," Michael agreed. Craig opened the folder he had placed on the table, fingered through a few pages before pulling out a spreadsheet and placing it on top of the pile. "Thank you for meeting with me so early this morning," Craig said. That was Craig's verbal cue that the meeting was officially starting. "Not a problem," Michael replied.

"First of all," Craig began, "let me begin by telling you how impressed I was when I saw the new billboard creative you did." Michael was a bit taken back by the praising comment, and it showed on his face. "Seriously," Craig reassured. "It was by far one of the best advertisements I've seen from you since you've been on board." "Thank you," Michael said, as he struggled to make sense of where the conversation was going. "From where I'm sitting, I think we should see some good quality leads come from that creative, and just in time too," Craig continued. "As I'm sure you know, sales have been down because the lead flow from your marketing department has dropped, not only in quantity but quality as well," Craig stated firmly. "Yes, sir, I know," Michael confirmed. Craig continued, "Look, we could have the best salespeople in the industry, but if they don't have the leads to work, we're dead in the water. We know the metrics, and we know how many leads each salesperson needs, we just have to produce them." Craig waited for an acknowledgment from Michael before continuing. "Understood," Michael said as his eyes dropped to the spreadsheet Craig was referencing.

Craig folded his hands, placed them on the pile of papers in front of him, looked directly at Michael and said, "I need you to understand that I'm disappointed that we even have to have this conversation, but it's imperative we get the lead flow back up to optimal levels." "I totally agree, Sir, that's why I worked so hard on the Billboard Creative," Michael injected. "And I understand that," Craig agreed. "That's why this is just a verbal conversation at this point. Nonetheless, I truly hope you understand how serious this situation is? We need leads at a certain level at all times, or the funnel just doesn't work. Do you understand?" Craig paused for a brief moment to let that statement sink in. Michael gave a single nod. "So, moving forward," Craig continued, "what can I do to help you?" "Well, I would truly value any advice you have," Michael stated genuinely. Craig thought for a moment about what he would do in Michael's situation. "I would challenge you to take another look at the other advertising channels we have running. Use that creative mind of yours, and revisit the internet and radio ads, and see if we can come up with something better." "I can do that!" Michael said confidently, while at the same time realizing he wasn't getting fired. "Good," Craig stated as he closed the folder in front of him "let's make it happen!" As they both stood up from the table, while pushing in their chairs, Craig added, "Oh, one more thing…". Michael turned to face Craig to hear his final point. "I want to thank you for the team you've put together. They're a tight-knit bunch, and it's clear they love working for you. You're a good leader, and it's one of the reasons I hired you." "Thank you," Michael replied, "they are a talented bunch."

Michael began to walk towards the office door. "Use them!" Craig suggested loudly. Michael stopped and turned towards Craig once again. "Sir?" Michael said, asking for clarification. "No one person has all the answers," Craig explained. "Some of the best ideas come from those on the front lines. You have an amazing team, so ask them what they think. Solicit their ideas. Lead them!" Michael smiled and nodded with acknowledgment. Now confident in his ability to get the job done, Michael left the office.

There is so much we can glean from Craig and Michael's short conversation. But, before we go breaking it down into details, let's look at the obvious. As I'm sure you've realized, Craig was a master at having those difficult conversations. As mentioned previously, no one likes to have these counseling sessions or, worse, right someone up. Nevertheless, they are a required element in the realm of Directorship. It's a skill you must master because I assure you, as a true leader, you will have plenty of these conversations throughout your career. The most effective and beneficial way to have these conversations is all in your approach. It's called the PCT Method or The Sandwich. Real leaders utilize this approach and has proven extremely beneficial at all levels. Whether you have to write-up a frontline employee or have that awkward conversation with your Director of Sales, the PCT method works. PCT is an acronym that stands for Praise, Challenge, and Thank. It's earned the nickname The Sandwich because you present the negative topic or point of discussion, in between two positive aspects. This approach is time-tested and very effective for a couple of reasons. Let's look at why Craig's conversation using this method was so successful:

1. <u>Performance Improvement</u>: Let's be honest: the whole reason for having these "conversations" is

that we want the team member to improve, right? As mentioned in the chapter on Mentorship, real leaders want those in their charge to be successful. If that's the case, the last thing you want to do is to demotivate someone or make them feel unvalued. I've seen too many times when a team member leaves their boss' office, believing their career at XYZ company is over and thinking they better get their resume out quickly! When this happens, I assure you the conversation did more harm than good. The fact of the matter is, this is a coaching session and should be treated as such. It's an opportunity for you as a leader to help direct or guide your team member towards success, not beat them down into the ground, like your scolding a child. Yes, there are times we need to be firm and very direct. However, when done correctly, the PCT Method does just that.

2. <u>End on a Positive Note</u>: I'm sure you've heard the phrase "Don't go to bed mad," or "never leave without saying goodbye" or words to that effect. The same reasoning applies here. Utilizing the PCT method not only ensures things end on a positive note, but it's also designed to go one step further, by motivating and encouraging as well! While the employee's shortcomings are directly addressed, this method ensures and promotes the fact that the employee is also a valued member of the team. They leave the office knowing precisely

what they have to do, feeling valued and appreciated, thus motivated to get the job done.

3. <u>It's Easier on You</u>: Last but not least, using the PCT method makes having these difficult conversations much easier on you. When you finally realize that these once uncomfortable situations are now opportunities for positive coaching and guidance, they become much more comfortable and more beneficial. In fact, don't be surprised if these sessions increase in number because you now understand the positive impact on the individual, the team, and the organization as a whole.

Dr. Phillip M. Randall is a fantastic business leader and a very respected mentor and confidante. He is an author, keynote speaker, lecturer, and Managing Partner at The Thorndike Group, a human capital consultancy specializing in individual and organizational effectiveness. When it comes to effective coaching, even during those difficult conversations, Randal (that's what he goes by, don't ever call him by his first name) teaches the following: "Real coaching is founded on igniting insight that is translated into meaningful action in order to help the recipient realize more of their potential. Let's break that down: When insight is ignited, the person who is stuck has an "aha" experience and learns something new. The good feeling that accompanies that learning, motivates the person to engage in the gritty kind of real-time, real-life learning that's needed to fully embrace new ways of thinking and doing things. That's the engine driving the lasting results that real coaching delivers".

As you can see, the PCT method is not only a great approach to addressing certain situations; it's a required skill all great leaders should master as part of their Directorship toolbox. Remember, the goal is to motivate and inspire, not to degrade, or even manipulate someone in a particular direction.

> CRITICAL NOTE: When you embrace the PCT Method, you gain the perspective of a true leader; a view far exceeding that of the average manager, while upgrading the overall performance of your leadership vessel in the process.

Improvement Plans and Terminations:

I would be remiss if I ended this chapter without at least discussing those dreaded Performance Improvement Plans (PIP's), and of course, the ultimate or final conversation of telling someone they're fired. Most managers cringe at even the thought of putting someone on a Performance Improvement Plan or God forbid, having to terminate someone. But here is the secret: Those cringing, nervy emotions are all caused by one's perception of the situation, stemming from, in large part, by how things were handled up to that point. Let me explain.

If you have been coaching and guiding your direct reports all along, including possible verbal warnings as in Craig and Michael's case, then placing someone on a Performance Improvement Plan or giving them a final warning or even terminating them, should not come as a surprise to the employee. Now, I'm not talking about a layoff or furlough, as those situations are most times unavoidable and unexpected. I'm talking about the situations we as leaders do have control over. In short, if you have done your job as a leader, trust me, the day you have to call someone into your office to fire them, I assure you, they will know what's coming.

> CRITICAL NOTE: An employee should NEVER be surprised by their termination. If they are, then we have failed them and ourselves as a leader.

One final note when it comes to performing terminations: Your goal should be to make the process as quick and painless as possible. That's right. When you call someone into your office to terminate them, the entire process should literally be less than five minutes, if not quicker.

I can't tell you the number of times I've witnessed terminations take 20 or 30 minutes or more. What should have been a quick conversation is sometimes elevated into an argument while the manager tries to explain why they are being fired. Some managers feel the need to spend an additional ten minutes expressing to the employee how much they regret terminating them, saying and "wishing things could have been different," etc. The longer you engage in a back and forth conversation with an employee, the greater chance you may say something you shouldn't. Look, I'm not saying you can't have compassion, or you have to be all stern like a teacher scolding a student, but the process should be quick. Again, this all stems back to how you've handled things previously that led up to this point of termination. If you have indeed done all you can to help your employees succeed, and it's still not working out, they will already know why they are being let go. There is no reason to have an extended conversation explaining the reasons why. For the longer you take, the more painful it becomes for the employee. It's already going to hurt; you can't avoid that, so don't make it any worse. Be professional, be compassionate, and be quick. It's better for everyone.

Directorship is an invaluable component when mastering the art of leadership. It's a critical compartment in your leadership vessel, yet many, even seasoned executives, still struggle with many of its facets. The key to successful Directorship is twofold.

Firstly, remember being proactive in dealing with difficult employee situations is vital, and will make future communications much easier in the process. Secondly, and even more importantly, successful Directorship requires one to understand its essential connection between the other leadership elements. In other words, successful Directorship requires Mentorship, Studentship, and the other "SHIPS," which we will be discussing in later chapters. Just as with an actual Navy combat ship, there are many, literally hundreds of compartments all designed and built to perform a specific task or function. However, only through working together, can a ship operate as a single entity and accomplish its mission. The Leadership Arena is no different. Are you beginning to see this "solidarity theme" becoming clearer?

As you know, for a company to be successful, people need to come together as a team to be effective, each group contributing in their own way to the mission or goal. Much in the same way, the Keel, the Hull, and all the other compartments of your leadership vessel must work in harmony. Each element, while separate in function, contributes to the success of the other.
When you can engage them all simultaneously, you have mastered the art of leadership.

LEADERSHIP LESSONS:

1. <u>Never Bite the Hand That Feeds You</u>: Most people understand that when you are promoted into a management position, it comes with an increase in salary accompanied by an increase in your day to day responsibilities. But it doesn't stop there. Always support the mission, vision and direction, even if you don't agree with it.

2. <u>Respect the Chain-of-Command</u>: Never go over your boss' head! There is only one reason you can and should go over your boss's head. In the case of illegal and/or unethical activity, such as sexual harassment or racial bias for example, it is not only your right, it is your responsibility to report it.
3. <u>Always Honor Your Values and Ethics:</u> There will most surely come a time in your career where your values or ethics, just don't match up with your employer's direction or the way they operate. In those situations, it's best to look for a new opportunity.
4. <u>Nepotism is Never a Good Idea</u>: In any organization that genuinely strives for a culture of solidarity, nepotism should not be allowed. As leaders, I believe we have a responsibility to educate others on the real effects it can have, and why such rules against nepotism should be more commonplace whenever possible.
5. <u>The PCT Method</u>: When you embrace the PCT Method, you gain the perspective of a true leader; a view far exceeding that of the average manager, while upgrading the overall performance of your leadership vessel in the process.

Chapter Six: PARTNERSHIP

"Real Leaders Recognize Success is a Team Effort!"

"Fire, Fire!" yelled Hanrahan in a panic as he quickly came up the ladder from the lower-level and approached the Top Watch. "It's smoking like crazy, and I'm not sure what's wrong!" Hanrahan yelled, sweat now beading and dripping from his forehead.

The Top Watch is what we called the person in charge of the engine room. Whether the ship was in-port or out to sea, someone was always "in charge" or the boss of a specific work shift. A shift, as it's commonly called in the civilian world, was known as a "watch" in the Navy. So, if you're assigned to be on duty for a specific shift, let's say from 0800-1200 (8 AM - 12 PM) you were considered to be on watch. If you were in charge of all those on watch, you were the "Top Watch." Petty Officer Phillips currently held that position.

"What's on Fire?" Phillips loudly asked as he stood up from his chair and grabbed the sound-powered phone in his right hand, ready to call in the emergency. "The Bilge Pump... I was working on it; it's smoking like crazy, I don't know why", Hanrahan answered, stuttering his words, obviously freaking out over the situation. "Dammit, Hanrahan!" Phillips scolded, slamming down the phone, and shaking his head in a 'here we go again' gesture. Now, smelling smoke, Phillips pushed Hanrahan out of the way and quickly made his way down the ladder, running past the smoking pump to the electrical control panel mounted on the bulkhead (wall). Phillips immediately turned the switch to the Off position. Hanrahan, who had followed Phillips down the ladder, let out a sigh of relief as the smoke from the pump almost immediately ceased.

Phillips turned around to face Hanrahan directly, giving him a stare that would frighten Mike Tyson. "Go to the upper level," Phillips began to order in a soft but firm voice "…and turn on the exhaust fans." Hanrahan, realizing once again he screwed up, nodded and began to head towards the upper level. "Can you do that without burning up something else?" Phillips added, purposely meaning to give Hanrahan another painful jab. Hanrahan, of course, didn't respond and continued on his way back to the upper level as ordered, engaging the exhaust fans to clear out what was left of the smoke. He took a seat next to the distilling plant, placing his elbows on his knees and resting his head in his hands. Of course, all this excitement caught the attention of the others in the engine room. This incident wasn't the first time Hanrahan had proven his lack of mechanical aptitude by breaking something. "Nice job," a fellow sailor sarcastically praised Hanrahan as he walked by. "You're really giving the rank "Fireman" a whole new meaning" called out another. "Knock it off!" Philips ordered with a yell as he reached the upper level, overhearing the teasing that was beginning to take place.

The term Fireman wasn't only a play on words, nor did it mean you were a firefighter as in the civilian sense. The term Fireman is an actual rank in the Navy. It meant Hanrahan was an E-3, having been promoted twice from his starting rank of E-1. You see, all jobs in the Navy are divided into one of three areas. Depending on your job description (Rating), you are either in the Seaman, Airman, or Fireman category. For example, if your job were to be a cook or what the Navy calls a Mess Management Specialist, you would start out as a <u>Seaman Recruit</u> (E-1). Then, your next promotion would be to a <u>Seaman Apprentice</u> (E-2), followed by the next rank of full <u>Seaman</u>. In Hanrahan's case, he started as a Fireman Recruit, then Fireman Apprentice, to then his current rank of Fireman. A Fireman was anyone who worked in the engineering field, including Boiler Technicians, Machinist Mates, and Damage Controlman, just to name a few. Of course, most obviously, an Airman was anyone who had a job associated with aircraft or aviation as a whole, such as an Air Traffic Controller, Aviation Ordinance, or Aviation Mechanic. Anyway, let's not get lost in the Navy's ranking structure. It would take an entire book to talk about the various ranks and job classifications in the Navy, especially when many claim the US Navy actually has a bigger air force than the entire US Air Force as a whole. That claim, however, is only

The Leadership Arena

valid when you include all aircraft of the U.S Marines in that total. Yes, the U.S. Marines are actually a part of the United States Navy, though most Marines don't like to talk about that.

A few hours later, Phillips walked into my office, closed the door behind him, and straddled a metal folding chair to face me, supporting his arms on the backrest. I had been selected to be the division's Career Counselor, so I had the luxury of a private air-conditioned office when I wasn't on watch. It was a nice added benefit in large contrast from the hot engine room that would easily reach about 110 degrees on a typical day. "We need to do something about Hanrahan," Phillips began. "Yeah, I heard what went down today. Any real Damage?" I asked. "Not really, he was attempting to stop a bilge pump from leaking and just tightened the seal a little too much, and POOF, smoke everywhere! He's just not mechanically inclined."

I sat back in my chair, crossed my arms, and turned in my chair to engage Phillips. "Looks like the ASVAB test didn't do its job in this case, huh?", I snickered. "Not at all," Phillips agreed. "I mean it's the Armed Services Vocational Aptitude Battery! Every branch uses it. It's designed to figure out what vocation one might be good at, but damn, they were way off on this one!" "What do you suggest we do?" I asked. "We can't fire him. He's ours for the next four years." Phillips continued, "but the other men are seriously giving him a hard time. They don't respect him, they don't want to hang out with him after hours, and that's not good for anyone, let alone the team." "No, it's not, you're right," I said. "but he's an amazingly hard worker. I mean, he gives 100%, he's never late, and if you ask him to stay late or take on extra things, he does it, no question."

Phillips nodded in agreement as his thoughts continued about how to solve the situation. "I have an idea," I stated very matter-of-factly. "What did we get on our last division birthing inspection?" A birthing is where we all slept and hung out in our off time. "Ten out of ten, a perfect score and the best we've had so far," Phillips replied. "And who was put in charge of getting the birthing ready for inspection?" I asked. I could almost see the light bulb above Phillips' head begin to glow. "It was Hanrahan, and it was his first time running the birthing." I looked directly at Phillips, and as we both smiled almost simultaneously, I added, "and I'll bet he can make a mean cup of coffee too!"

Job Alignment – You Can Hire Talent, But You Can't Hire Loyalty!

One of the first skills you must develop in the realm of Partnership is what I call job Aligning. A closely related and commonly known term in the corporate world is Job Alignment, sometimes called Role Alignment. There will be many explanations and different facets to what's widely called Job Alignment if you do an internet search on the definition. However, the definition of Job Aligning, as it relates to The Leadership Arena, is to <u>ensure the experiences, skills, and talents of your team member meet or exceed the required skills and abilities of their job or position</u>. In other words, are they a good fit for the position and the functions they must perform to be successful? More importantly, and the main focus of Job Alignment is, what does a real leader do in a situation when they are not a good fit? What do you do when you have an exemplary employee, loyal and hard-working to the core, who's having difficultly performing some aspects of the job? Unfortunately, too many times, when this happens, the poor managing "leader" simply begins the administrative process to replace the employee. To this type of manager, it's the only option they know of because "it must have been a poor hiring decision" in their minds.

On SHRM.org, (the Society of Human Resource Management), was an article titled 'Alignment Is Essential to Effective Performance and Profitability.' In this article printed back in July of 2011 by Robert P. Hewes and Alan M. Patterson, it read: "It is easy to blame people for poor execution. After all, they are the ones doing the work. Sometimes there are clear situations in which an individual is not a fit for the job or needs more training and development to be effective. However, what about situations where you have dedicated, hard-working people working with inefficient, bloated, or cumbersome processes? This is a process problem, not a people problem."

Additionally, and even more importantly, I'll ask the question again: What do you do with that same hard-working, dedicated and loyal individual, once you justly conclude, they're just the wrong person for that specific job? What do you do when working ethic, loyalty, and character are exemplary, but they fall short in performing required job functions? Well, it all comes down to this. Here is the secret to Job Aligning and why it's so essential to master this element of leadership: The impact of a poor hiring decision, is nothing compared to the effects of losing a great employee.

> CRITICAL NOTE: You can hire personality, you can hire skill, you can even hire talent, but you can't hire LOYALTY!

I have had the opportunity to work for some fantastic leaders, and most will tell you, if they run across someone with amazing talent, combined with an impeccable work ethic, they will find a position for that person if possible, even if they have to create one. On the flip side, I've seen situations where an amazingly loyal and hard-working employee was let go because they were struggling with a few of their job-related tasks. If someone is highly valued, isn't it worth the time to see if there is a much better fit within the organization before you decide to toss them out? Real Leaders do this because they understand the invaluable asset they have in a person with that kind of dedication and commitment. It's an investment in human capital (which we'll discuss a little later). For example, let's revisit the story of Hanrahan discussed earlier.

I learned the art of Job Aligning very early in my naval career, but it wasn't by choice. Let me explain. In the US Navy, and I'll venture to say even in the entire US military, the phrase "You're Fired" does not exist. When someone is assigned to your ship, squadron, platoon, division, whatever, they are filling a required position set by the Department of the Navy.
This required position is called a billet. In other words, in the case of Hanrahan, the Department of the Navy knows how many people are needed to run a particular ship or naval base successfully. They know how many engineers, cooks, quartermasters, boatswains, pilots, etc. it takes to run that command. Once a position or billet is filled, they are generally assigned to that billet for a specific period of time, typically between two to four years. So, if someone new is assigned to your division like Hanrahan, you can't just fire them because you're unhappy with their performance. You've got to make it work! Even if someone would commit something more serious like get into a physical fight or show up for work still under the influence of alcohol, you can't just say, "you're fired." You can write them up, or what the military calls putting someone on report, but even in those cases, (except for serious felony crimes) you're still stuck with them. They may be demoted in rank or get half their pay docked for a couple of months, even restricted to the ship for 30 days, but they are still assigned to your department.

With Hanrahan, you may be thinking that he spent the rest of his time making bunks, and stripping and waxing floors, instead of performing the duties as an engineer as his billet would indicate. However, that wasn't the case at all. In fact, the decision to put him in charge of the birthing worked out perfectly. You see, it wasn't that Hanrahan didn't have any mechanical aptitude, he just needed more time and training than most to gain the essential skills. Hey, we all learn in different ways and at different speeds, right? Additionally, being responsible for the birthing was extremely important for many reasons. Firstly, if your birthing failed inspection, liberty (time off) for all who occupied that space could be put on hold until the birthing was brought up to par and re-inspected. So, passing inspection every time was important to everyone looking forward to going home to their families at the end of the workday.

Secondly, because Hanrahan was the perfect fit for the job, no one ever worried about passing birthing inspections going forward. This relieved pressure and extra time allowed the team to focus on the "To-Do's" in the engine room. Consequently, the team actually gained a huge respect for Hanrahan. So much so, they actually started tutoring him in the engine room, and in no time, Hanrahan became a confident, well-respected member of the engineering team. You see, in that type of environment, you can't help but to genuinely look for the best in people.

> CRITICAL NOTE: To continuously seek to match one's strengths with challenging positions in which they will excel, is job Alignment at its finest. It's a leadership trait, not an event.

I presented this true story because it speaks to much more than just teamwork. Through Job Aligning, partnerships were formed within the department, thus strengthening the team overall. Though the solution was crafted and somewhat imposed, nonetheless, it blossomed into a beneficial "I'll scratch your back, you scratch mine" result. It's a clear example of Job Alignment and the stark differences between management and leadership. Through these small internal partnerships, you lay the groundwork for each team member's individual success, and ultimately the success of your team and organization.

Human Capital – The Line Item of the Future.

Okay, so what exactly is Human Capital? And why is it so important that I include the topic in a book about leadership, let alone in a chapter on partnerships? The last thing I want to do is turn this book into one of those over-technical MBA or "business guru" type books. I'm not here to try to impress you with an extended vocabulary, or by including Harvard-level business terminology and theories. That's just not my style, though I may pull in a cool quote from time to time, [Smile]. I include it in this book for two crucial reasons. One, I believe the real leader of tomorrow, will realize Human Capital, while not a line item on any balance sheet, is a crucial ingredient to the success of the people they lead and organizations they manage. Two, as you will soon see, it takes a genuine partnership between you and your subordinate to manage human capital effectively.

If you try to find a standard definition of Human Capital, you'll get a wide range of explanations, but almost all point to one central theme or theory. I like the best description by Will Kenton in May 2019 in an article titled Human Capital on Investopedia.com. It's to the point, well-defined, and by far the best explanation I have found. He writes, "Human capital is an intangible asset or quality not listed on a company's balance sheet. It can be classified as the <u>economic value of a worker's experience and skills</u>. This includes assets like education, training, intelligence, skills, health, and other things employers value, such as loyalty and punctuality. The concept of human capital recognizes that <u>not all labor is equal</u>. But employers can improve the quality of that capital by <u>investing in employees</u>—the education, experience, and abilities of employees all have economic value for employers and the economy as a whole. Human capital is substantial because it's perceived to increase productivity and, thus, profitability."

<u>It's What Leaders Do Naturally:</u> Did the proverbial lightbulb go off in your head? If not, read that paragraph again, please. As you can see, since page one of this

book, we've been talking about Human Capital and how to improve it all along. We just didn't use the technical term. Again, your priority as a leader is to help those in your charge become successful. To do that, you improve human capital through continuous personal and professional development. Through mentorship, studentship, and the like, all lend themselves to effective Human capital management. The more you invest in your employees, the more valuable and productive they become. The more useful and productive they become, translates into stable profitability. It is the ultimate "win-win-win" situation in the corporate arena. Right now, as you are reading this book, you are increasing your skills and knowledge. By doing so, you are increasing your value to the organization, thus increasing the organization's overall human capital.

> CRITICAL NOTE: Solid Employee + Continuous Development = Increased Human Capital

Even things outside your job description can increase or decrease human capital. For example, let's say you have two employees, each equal in their administrative abilities. However, one of them is in good health, and the other is average to below-average health, causing frequent absences. That good health is valuable to an organization and thus increases its human capital. For those of you who read The Executive Arena, the first book in the Arena Trilogy, do you remember the phrase "being good at your job is only half the battle"? That phrase rings true here and shines additional light on the importance of managing this line item of the future.

Believe it or not, this human capital concept is nothing new and has been around for hundreds of years. The military's ranking system is a textbook example. Your rank in the military is a direct reflection of the value you bring to the organization. For instance, in the Navy, in order to get promoted, many things must transpire and align before one is advanced or promoted in rank. Take a close look at the following; it's genuinely a brilliant method for human capital management.

1. <u>Time in Service:</u> Before one is even considered for promotion, they must spend a specific length of time at their current rank. The military calls it Time in Service and simply ensures one has acquired the necessary "Experience."
2. <u>Advancement Exam:</u> To get promoted, one must also take an academic exam, related to their specific rating (job). For example, a Boiler Technician looking to advance from a 3rd Class Petty Officer (E-4) to 2nd Class Petty Officer (E-5) they are required to pass the advancement exam for E-5 Boiler Technicians. Additionally, their test scores are all matched against everyone else taking the exam. If 10,000 people are taking the E-5 Boiler Technician exam, but the Navy only needs 600, only the top 600 will be promoted. This

ensures those promoted have acquired the necessary "Skills."

3. <u>Evaluations and Recommendation:</u> If one has the required time-in-service and feels he or she is ready to take the advancement exam, the next step is to officially "request permission" to advance or take the exam. Getting permission to take the exam is the second step in the process, but I put it third on this list for a good reason. If your superiors don't think you are ready for the next level, your request can be denied. The request form that you submit must be signed by everyone in your chain of command, typically about four to five signatures. The decision to approve or disapprove one's request is based on both their performance evaluations and frankly your overall behavior. You may be smart and good at your job, but if you have issues with punctuality, or you've gotten into trouble a few times for being disrespectful, you may be "passed-over" for that specific exam cycle. And by the way, that exam is only given once a year. This evaluation and recommendation step is to ensure acceptable "Work ethic and Character."

There you have it. The Navy's entire advancement structure is designed and built around the management of human capital. The higher your Experience, Skills, Work ethic, and Character, the higher value you bring to the organization. Thus, you are rewarded for the increased value you bring through promotions, pay, and increased responsibility. What does one do once they are promoted? Well, the system is designed to continuously entice and support your path to the next level. When I decided to become a Company Commander (RDC), billets like that are considered vital to the Navy's mission. Because of this, you're rewarded with extra points on all future advancement exams. It's kind of like getting extra credit for a project; only the project is called human capital. As you can see, there is a method to the madness, a reason for every season, and an end goal for everything the Navy (and military) does. And it works just as effectively in the corporate world if you dare take the lead and embrace its practices.

Embracing Human Resources as a Business Partner

A Brief History: History tells us that a gentleman by the name of John R. Commons, an economist back in the 1890s, was the first to coin the term Human Resources in a book he published titled, "The Distribution of Wealth." However, the actual practice or the idea of human resources as a viable part of business success began with two entrepreneurs. Robert Owen (1771-1858) and Charles Babbage (1791-1871), during the industrial revolution, realized some fascinating facts. Now, I have to admit, when you first hear the following statement, it can be viewed as a "well duh" moment, almost comedic in a sense, but nevertheless, it must be told. Robert and Charles concluded that happy employees were more productive than unhappy ones. They believed that to increase productivity; it would be better to find ways to motivate employees versus threatening them in some way. [You Think? I told you it was funny.]

It wasn't until about a century later that Human Resources actually became a field of study. As time went on, and world wars played a crucial role in the development of manufacturing jobs and the wide-spread creation of workers unions, the HR Department quickly became more commonplace. Its importance became even more solidified as new legislation for worker safety, and fair treatment was continuously voted into law and continues even today.

<u>The HR Leader of Tomorrow:</u> Unfortunately, because of how Human Resources originated and had developed in the early years, the perception some have today of HR is either not a positive one, or they simply don't realize HR's actual function and value. It's not uncommon for frontline employees to actually fear being called to the HR office, or even management personnel getting nervous when the Director of HR calls to inquire about an employee complaint. Additionally, some too many senior executives view the role of HR as merely transactional, something the company is "required to have" if you run a decent-sized business. Well, I hate to say this, but if you are one of those type individuals, you may find yourself choking on the dust of your competition as they fly past you in market share. Because regardless of the type and scope of your organization, tomorrow's leaders will see Human

Resources as their business partner, not just a transactional / required-by-law department.

That said, if Human Resource Management is your chosen vocation, your career success as a leader will rely in large part upon your ability to perform more strategically in your field.

> CRITICAL NOTE: HR leaders of tomorrow will procure that seat at the boardroom table because they are perceived as a vital line position within the company, who's contributions have a direct and positive impact on the company's bottom line, overall growth, and success of the organization.

Glenn Llopis, a Forbes.com contributor, spoke to this very thing in an article titled, "HR Departments Must Urgently Become Human Capital Departments" back in 2018. Glenn writes, "…Human resources – in an age when the individual defines the business rather than the business defining the individual – doesn't just need a strategy for evolution. It needs a complete shift in mindset from top to bottom; from human resources to human capital and resources. The alignment HR needs to drive is between individual capabilities and what the role in an organization those capabilities can solve for. The problem is organizations try to align those capabilities with job titles and functions. The difference between the function and what it solves for is the difference between <u>human resources</u> and <u>human capital</u>. That's why the term human capital is so important. Human capital is how people contribute to growth. It is about allowing the individual to influence more. The individual needs to define the business – and thus should define the work that HR does."

I think we can all agree that today's working environment is vastly different from 20 years ago, and it's continuously evolving. For example, I remember when having a home office was a luxury that only afforded to the most senior executives. Yet today, organizations are beginning to realize a "work-from-home" option, even if in only during an emergency, might just be a necessity. As I'm writing this very sentence, we are smack dab in the middle of the Covid19 outbreak. Businesses are still closed, and the economy is suffering. However, I have noticed that those companies that have the ability and have embraced the technology while trusting in their employee to get the job done are far less affected by the mandated shutdowns. Additionally, many studies have proven that 4-day work weeks are much more productive, and people are much happier. Yet, most organizations can't get past the idea of giving employees three days off. Amazon has adopted the 4-day work week, and I assure you it's by design.

The leaders of tomorrow... no, the leaders of today must embrace the human element, and Human Resources will be the ones leading that charge in the most successful organizations. Glenn goes on to say, "HR can't just be a compliance cop protecting the company from those pesky employees. It must empower employees who want to help grow the company and evolve to achieve their goals, too. In addition, HR can't just be about data either. Not everything human can be optimized through data – and looking at the data is no replacement for having insight and <u>listening to people</u>. That's what's getting lost in all these discussions of HR: people! Humans, like employees, are a group – a species if you will. Something to be studied, controlled, defined. People are individuals. We can't forget about the people."

CRITICAL NOTE: Within the most successful organizations, HR will be leading the charge to humanize our businesses. Perhaps leading that charge, should also come with a newly renamed department: "Human Capital Management and Resources."

<u>The Mentor and Coach to Your Leaders:</u> We have already discussed how being a lifelong learner (studentship) is critical to your success as a leader, and how studentship is just as crucial to your subordinates. But where does one turn for leadership and management advice while on the job? If you run an organization, where do those in management roles, go for guidance and assistance dealing with personnel management issues? Where does one turn for leadership training and improvement? The answer, once again, is Human Resources!

The Leadership Arena

This is a department whose entire function is that of human capital management, meaning their whole mission is the individual and organizational improvement and growth. HR is not the enemy; they are your business partner! Unfortunately, there are still plenty of those so-called "leaders" at the top of many organizations that still have that transactional mindset. Just look at the standard definition found through a basic internet search on "What is Human Resources?" The result and I'm paraphrasing because I don't want to bash any specific articles or organizations is as follows: <u>Human resources: a department responsible for finding, screening, recruiting, and training job applicants, and administering employee-benefit programs. As a company grows, HR plays a role in helping manage a changing environment and the higher demand for quality employees</u>. I'm sorry, but to me, that sounds like the definition of a recruiting firm, (aside from the benefits portion). And therein lies the problem.

Real leaders understand the true value of HR, and they utilize them whenever possible. If you are the President or CEO of an organization, you should encourage, if not demand, that your leadership team take advantage of this vital coaching and mentoring resource, because that's exactly what HR is - a vital resource! From simple daily advice on how to handle an emotional employee during a termination, to more sophisticated strategies like improving or building strong interdepartmental relationships, your HR department is the key to organizational growth and success.

You know, it's been said many times that it's the people behind an organization that makes it successful. If that's the case, then as leaders, I believe it's our responsibility to correct the inaccurate perceptions our employees may have of Human Resources by creating a real business partnership with a department and industry that is truly "all about the people." Mark my words, the most successful companies of tomorrow will widely embrace the HR element and its managing of human capital.

The Social Capital Theory

Okay, not to throw another capital theory at you, but I really believe you're going to like this one. In my last book, The Executive Arena, we discussed in detail the importance of networking, and how improving the quality of those you associate with will have a positive impact on your career. In other words, if you want to be a successful executive, then you need to hang around other successful executives. We talked about how you need to align yourself with others who share your ambitions, or at the very least, share your level of aspiration. Well, now we are going to take that networking concept to a whole new level. Are you ready?

Social Capital is an area of study within social science and a topic that is growing in popularity. In your spare time, if you'd like to do your own research on Social Capital, I urge you to do so. It's a vast and fascinating topic, but for the purpose of The Leadership Arena, particularly this chapter on Partnership, we're going to keep this very straightforward. Simply put, <u>Social Capital is the value one receives directly from social networks, allowing individuals to achieve things they usually couldn't do by themselves</u>. I teach the fact that, "Social Capital extends your reach and ability through people!" Again, it's the age-old phrase "no one becomes successful on their own," but at a whole new level.

Additionally, with social capital comes the benefit of reciprocity or the win-win scenario. A great example of social capital in action is a Neighborhood Watch Program. Let's say while on vacation, your neighbor calls the police because they noticed someone snooping around your back yard. You were not there, but because of the social network you are a part of, you received the benefit or value. It's the value you personally gain from your community having someone always on patrol, thus reducing the crime rate in your neighborhood.

Today, this concept of continuous involvement in social networks is on the rise, and for very good reason. Organizations like Network After Work, Eventbrite, and Meetup.com are growing in popularity because of the vast array of benefits one can receive from merely showing up.

These are fantastic networking opportunities where like-minded professionals come together, have a glass of wine (or your favorite beverage), and exchange great conversations with business cards all within a couple of hours. The benefits you can gain might be as simple as a dining recommendation for some great seafood, or as significant as finding your next Director of Sales or finally landing that super-large account you've been after for months.

No other industry understands the real power of Social Networks more than those involved in Risk Management and Employee-benefits Brokerage. Within this industry, there are a select few (the most successful of course) who have business models built around honest and genuine relationship building. It's part of their DNA. Companies like M.E. Wilson headquartered in Tampa, Florida, are perfect examples of Social Network Management at its finest. They host formal and informal networking events, educational seminars, and more all designed to support studentship while enhancing Social Capital. They understand that success requires more than just community attendance; it's about individual support and community involvement. Of course, every company hopes to spawn new opportunities from hosting events like this. But to people-centric organizations like M.E. Wilson as an example, landing a new account is a byproduct of their ongoing commitment to the communities they serve, and the partnerships they cultivate.

As leaders, it's not only essential to understand the power social capital can have on our success, but we also need to ensure those we lead genuinely appreciate the advantages social networks can have on their success, and thus the success of the organizations that employ us. In summary, get out and network. Be a part of these social groups that help people and teach others to do the same! But do so, because you genuinely want to help others and the communities in which you live, not because you're looking for your next sale.

> CRITICAL NOTE: Don't waste your time focusing on success! Focus on helping others, and success will show up all on its own.

LEADERSHIP LESSONS:

1. Job Aligning, as it relates to The Leadership Arena is to ensure the experiences, skills and talents of your team member, aligns with the required skills and talents of their job or position.
2. To continuously seek to match one's strengths with challenging positions in which they will excel, is Job Aligning at its finest. It's a leadership trait, not an event.
3. You can hire personality, you can hire skill, you can even hire talent, but you can't hire LOYALTY!
4. Human Capital is the economic value of a worker's experience and skills. This includes assets like education, training, intelligence, skills, health, and other things employers' value such as loyalty and punctuality.

5. The Navy's entire advancement structure is designed and built around the management of human capital. The greater your Experience, Skills, Work ethic and Character, the greater value you bring to the organization.
6. HR leaders of tomorrow will procure that seat at the boardroom table, because they will become a vital line position within the company, who's contributions have a direct and positive impact on the company's bottom line, and thus the overall growth and success of the organization.
7. Social Capital is the value one receives directly from social networks, allowing individuals to achieve things they normally couldn't do by themselves. It extends your reach and ability through people!

Chapter Seven: OWNERSHIP

January 7th, 1989 – A Quiet Day at the Office?

As you might imagine, almost every day of recruit training or boot camp is all hustle and bustle. For eight long weeks, each day is jampacked with things to do and schedules to meet. There are academic classes to attend, physical training sessions to accomplish, "Drill" practice, and constant inspections on just about everything a recruit would touch. Drill was a term used for practicing how to march as well as other various military movements, like Attention, Parade Rest, Present Arms, and other must-learn actions and commands. One interesting fact is that from day one of recruit training, "drill" unbeknownst to the recruits, was in all actuality, practicing for graduation. The Navy's recruit graduation ceremony is quite impressive and takes weeks of practice to perfect it – well, eight weeks to be exact. So, its preparation begins the day recruits arrive for boot camp. Again, the recruits don't realize this until about week six, well into their training; another "ah-ha" or Karate Kid moment.

So, as you can see, a working day at Recruit Training Command, Great Lakes Illinois, is never-ending. One could almost conclude that keeping the recruits busy was by design. I mean, while any military boot camp can be physically demanding, in the Navy, it is far more emotionally demanding vs. physical, and allowing too much time for recruits to dwell on a specific situation wasn't healthy either. However, there was one exception. From time to time, the Company Commander would allow some well-deserved "free-time" for the recruits to, as we would say, "catch their breath." Today was one of those days.

It was a Saturday afternoon, so the recruit's schedule was open, which meant there were no scheduled events, and the Company Commander (CC) could utilize that time as they saw fit. My partner needed the day off to attend a family wedding, so I offered to hold down the fort while he had some fun for the weekend. It was commonplace and acceptable to "switch-off" each Saturday or Sunday so the other CC can have some time to rest up. Of course, that didn't happen unless you had a senior company, which meant they were at least in their 6th week of training.

I won't lie; being a Company Commander was extremely demanding, which is why not many sailors volunteered for that billet. At a minimum, your hours were from 4 AM to 10 PM, seven days a week, for eight consecutive weeks. You held this scheduled until you trained three companies in total (about 24 weeks), at which time you were placed in what the Navy called a "hold-job." A hold-job was basically a position on base with standard or regular working hours, which could be anything from some administrative job pushing papers, to even conducting inspections. This hold job, generally about four to six weeks, was to give Company Commanders some return to normalcy for a while, before going back to training recruits. It was clearly a Navy attempt to block burnout or, at the very least, prevent you from kicking the dog, or a family member when you were able to be home.

On a serious note, the divorce rate for Company Commanders was around 75% for obvious reasons. During Company Commander School, many of us waved-off that statistic, with skeptical phrases like "Yeah right, I'm not worried," and "My marriage is strong," only to be proven wrong within a year. Unfortunately, I was one that added to that very real statistic.

Today being a Saturday, I allotted the better part of the afternoon for the recruits to do what they please. As I gazed out through my office picture window overlooking the barracks, I took notice of some of the recruits sitting on the floor in the direct sunlight gleaming in through the windows. I couldn't help but think of a house cat trying to catch some rays because they weren't allowed to go outside. I'm guessing it felt pretty good, because as beautiful as it may have looked from the inside looking out, the weather here in January can be quite deceiving. It was about 1300 hours (1 PM), and the temperature outside had already climbed a pleasant 14 degrees Fahrenheit. The winds were calm today, so the windchill was only at -1 degrees. It was a welcoming change from last week's -30 degrees wind chill factor.

I had just poured myself another cup of coffee and was watching some recruits polishing their shoes, others writing letters home, just a relaxing day at the office when I heard the compartment watch yell out firmly, "Attention on Deck!" So much for a relaxing day at the office, I thought to myself. With coffee still in hand, I walked out of my office to meet the visitor, who was obviously someone of importance by the reaction of the compartment watch. I turned to look down the corridor towards the compartment entrance, to find Chief Daniels approaching me, in what seemed like in a panic. The Compartment watch followed protocol and began to sound off "Sir, Seamen Jones, company..." "Shut up, Rick," Daniels interrupted, "not now! Go back to your station!"

Chief Daniels was the Company Commander for company 024, another company in the same graduating class as us, located right across the hall. "What's up?" I asked, now easily verifying the panic in his voice. Before he answered, Daniels quickly turned his head to look over his shoulder towards the entrance as if to make sure he wasn't followed. "MED is in the house," he began, "Surprise inspection. I wanted to give you a heads up". "On a Saturday, are you kidding me?" I asked, eyes-wide-open, now feeling the anxiety begin to build in myself. Daniels slapped me on the shoulder, and as he headed for the door, exclaimed, "Yeah, baby, good luck!" "Thanks

The Leadership Arena

for the heads up! I owe you one!" I replied. I quickly shuffled into my office, spilling a bit of coffee as I set the cup down on my desk, then headed out to address the recruits.

The recruits, now scattered about the compartment, were all still standing at attention. No one ever gave the command to "carry -on" after the attention on deck command, so there they stood, stiff as a board and in complete silence. This position worked out for the better because I needed their undivided attention, and I needed it quickly. "Listen up, everyone," I ordered. "MED is doing surprise inspections in the building, and there's a good chance they may pay us a visit. We can't allude to the fact that we had a heads-up, so, when I say go, I need you all to quietly and calmly make sure your lockers and bunks are in order, and the compartment doesn't have any major infractions." I paused for a few seconds to make sure my orders had sunk in, then softly gave the command, "Go." As ordered, the recruits began to tidy up the compartment and tend to their lockers and bunks if needed.

During a surprise inspection, specifically in the middle of the day, MED couldn't inspect anyone's personal appearance, like ensuring they were clean-shaven or in clean uniforms. However, the condition of the barracks, like the deck (floors), the head (showers and toilets), as well as the washroom (where we scrubbed belts, leggings, and other military uniform accessories) was open game. These things should always be in top-notch condition unless they were currently in use. Though I knew we were in good shape, I still hoped MED was on a different mission that didn't include us and would simply pass by. I headed back to my office with my fingers virtually crossed. "Attention on Deck!" sounded the compartment watch again. So much for wishful thinking.

As I headed out of my office to greet the inspector, I recognized him immediately. It was petty officer Johnson, a fellow Company Commander, who was obviously on a hold-job with MED. "How's your day going, Spector?" he asked as he held out his hand. "It was going great until now," I replied as we conducted the customary handshake. The handshake was more of a "passing control" gesture from one to the other. MED, though only temporary, was now in control of my company. "Don't worry," Johnson assured, "we are just checking Heads and Washrooms today, no Compartments or Lounges." "That'll work," I replied. Johnson ordered the recruits to muster in front of their bunks and remain at parade rest during the inspection. I followed Johnson into the head, and the compartment watch followed me with his notebook and pen in hand to document any infractions the inspector finds. We were in the head for all of about 10 seconds when Johnson reported "Looks good" and turned to leave, no doubt making his way towards the washroom.

This 10-second flyby was a good sign because, believe me, if MED wanted to find something wrong, they could. It meant that unless there was a blatant infraction, the inspector wasn't going to look very hard. He was just going through the motions.

The Leadership Arena

As Johnson approached the washroom, he reached for the handle and pulled the door open. And there, as bright as day (literally), was the blatant infraction. The washroom lights were left on, a huge "no-no" in the world of recruit training. Johnson turned his head to look at me, with a 'you know I have to write this up' glare. "If it helps," Johnson began apologetically, "I won't look any further." "I appreciate it," I replied, darn well knowing it didn't matter if they found something else wrong or not.

Johnson tore off the top sheet of his inspection pad, handed it to me, and left the barracks. We officially failed the surprise inspection. As I stood there holding the inspection results in my hand, there were only two questions on my mind. Who in the hell left the lights on, and what was I going to do about it? Just then, one of the recruits yelled out, "Attention on deck!" "Jesus Christ, now what?" I mumbled to myself as I headed for the compartment entrance. It was Chief Daniels. "Carry on Rick," he called out as he signaled with a nod to meet in my office. It was time for a private conversation.

"Did you get hit"? Daniels asked. By hit, he meant did we have any major infractions. "Oh yeah, washroom lights on. How about you?" I asked. Daniels replied with his favorite phrase, "Yeah, baby! Two unflushed toilets." I shook my head, still in disbelief that our quiet day at the office was quickly turning into another "teachable moment." "I think we should get the two companies together and make it rain," Daniels suggested. I nodded slowly in agreement and replied, "Why not? But I need to do something first - want to take a ride?"

Daniels smiled with a grin from ear to ear. "Ownership?" he asked as he opened my office door. As we both headed out of the office, I answered his question with the words he would appreciate most, "Yeah, baby!"

The day it Rained Indoors!

About 30 minutes had passed since Daniels, and I left the barracks. I'm sure the recruits were wondering what was going on during our absence since we said nothing about the now, well-known failed inspection. I've always believed it was beneficial to let recruits ponder certain situations, providing them an opportunity to deduce amongst themselves what went wrong and how to solve a problem. To me, this somewhat-forced problem-solving builds teamwork and comradery, once again through conditioning. More than just physical training and academic classes, recruit training presents real-life situations, genuine teachable moments, in a safe, controlled environment. In most cases, recruits learn the valuable lesson all on their own, which is truly the genius of how boot camp is structured. However, there are other times when the Company Commander can step in when an opportunity presents itself, to ensure a valuable lesson is absorbed and retained. This was one of those opportunities.

The Leadership Arena

Chief Daniels parked the car, and I grabbed the bag of McDonald's take out, as well as the three drinks that were placed in the cardboard cup carrier. As soon as I opened the car door, the blast of frigged air literally took my breath away. Even though you are constantly reminded how cold outside it truly is, the bright sun and blue sky can catch you off guard every single time. One would think being born and raised in Chicago; you'd be used to the nasty weather, but you never really do. I don't care where you live when it's friggin' cold; it's cold.

As we approached the rear entrance to the barracks, moving as quickly as we could, being careful not to slip on an unexpected sheet of ice, Daniels rushed ahead and opened the door for me since my hands were full. I let out a sigh of relief as I stepped into the well-heated corridor to the barracks. This blast of air, in contrast to the previous, was like opening an oven door set at 450 degrees but much more welcoming. Daniels quickly pulled the door closed behind him, fighting against the hydraulic shocks trying to slow his progress. "Yeah, baby, that's cold!" Daniels exclaimed as the door sealed shut. "Another day in paradise," I added. "Five minutes?" Daniels asked. "How about ten?" I responded, "it will give me time to get things set up." "Ten it is. See you in a few".

The Compartment Watch sounded off again, as I entered the compartment. Even before everyone could get to attention, I yelled, "Everyone in front of your bunks!" Understanding exactly what I wanted, the recruits scurried to get into inspection formation. This consisted of each recruit standing in front of their perspective bunks, at attention, facing the center of the compartment. In other words, each side of the compartment both Port (left side) and Starboard (right side) would be facing each other. There was complete silence as I walked to the head of the compartment to address the company. I placed the bag of McDonald's down on the first table in front of me and slid the drinks next to the bag, so the recruits could get a good look at the treasure I had brought back from my excursion.

"Alright," I began. "I'm sure by now; everyone knows the results of our surprise inspection." So, I am only going to ask this once, and one time only". I paused as I could see their bodies stiffen as they waited for the obvious question. "I want to know… which one of you left the washroom lights on?" I again paused for effect. "Whoever is brave enough to admit it, please step forward," I ordered. As I stared out at the two perfect lines of recruits stretching fore and aft (from front to back), none of them moved a muscle. Then came a surprising voice from behind me. "I did, Sir!" I turned around to find the Compartment Watch, Seaman Recruit White, had stepped forward. "You did?" I asked for clarification. "Yes, Sir," he answered. "When I made my rounds, I must have left them on. It's my fault, Sir."

White was one of those recruits who was having a difficult time with boot camp. He wasn't the sharpest tool in the shed, so he struggled academically, and his

The Leadership Arena

inspection results were lacking, to say the least, including this one. The situation was perfect. "Well, I'm sorry to hear that White," I began to explain. "But you know what? It's not your fault. It's not your fault that you've been struggling a bit in class, or that you have a hard time getting your bunk made correctly." The compartment was still motionless and silent, with the exception of my voice. "So here's what we are going to do. When I say go, everyone will push your bunks back, and then I want everyone lined up on the Starboard side, facing the center of the compartment. Ready, Go!"

Pushing their bunks back meant they would move them outward towards the sides of the compartment. This evolution provided more floor space in the center of the compartment to do exercises, stencil uniforms, teach lessons or other activities where extra floor space and an unobstructed view would be beneficial.

Just as the recruits began to line up on one side, Seaman Recruit White sounded off again. "Attention on Deck!" This time I know who it was. "Carry on, Rick!" Daniels yelled. Following Chief Daniels into my compartment was his entire company in a single file line. "Port-side!" Daniels ordered his recruits as he pointed towards the now empty side of the compartment. When the recruits were all lined up, we put them at attention and continued with the lesson.

"White," I called out. "Come here, right now." White quickly came front and center, went to attention, and responded, "Yes, Sir!" "As I mentioned before," I began, ensuring my voice was now loud enough for all to hear, "it's not your fault that we failed the inspection. So, I want you to sit here, take a load off, and enjoy this wonderful lunch, while Chief Daniels and I take care of the real problem." "No, thank you, Sir!" White immediately responded. "That wasn't a question, Recruit!" I demanded with an even louder tone and pointed to the head table. White took a seat. "Daniels?" I said. "The floor is yours!" "Kozinski and Jefferies, front and center!" Daniels called out. Two recruits stepped out of line, and we told them to sit at the table with White. "Everyone else," I instructed, "DROP!"

Immediately, the recruits dropped into the push-up position, holding their bodies up with their arms and waiting for the next order. With now close to 170 men in a single compartment designed for about 80-90 maximum, there wasn't much room to exercise, even with the bunks pushed back. We left them in the up position while we addressed the three recruits who had failed the inspection. "Hey, guys," Daniels began with a friendly tone towards the three, now nervously sitting at the table, "dig in!" I dug into the bag of McDonald's and began placing burgers and fries in front of each of the three recruits. "We're serious," I added, "we want you to enjoy this moment." "Yeah, so eat up! I don't want to see any food leftover," Daniels instructed genuinely with a smile.

I looked out at the sea of sailors (pun intended), noticing some of their arms beginning to shake as they struggled to keep themselves in the push-up position. "I almost forgot about the others," I said jokingly to Daniels. "Down!" I yelled out. You could hear the apparent sigh of relief as they all lowered their bodies, releasing a burst of air as their chest hit the floor. I gave them about 2 seconds to rest in the down position then gave the command "Up!" The sea of sailors rose again to the up position.

This evolution lasted for about 10 minutes until we decided to switch to sit-ups for an additional 15 minutes. This was followed by other standard exercises like jumping jacks to get the recruits "warmed up" before the real strenuous activities began, like Sharks, for example. During Sharks, the recruits would lay on their bellies with their arms straight out in front of them, like they were flying. When the Company Commander yelled Shark, the recruits would lift both their legs and arms and beginning moving them quickly up and down like you were swimming. The only thing touching the floor was your belly or midsection. It was excruciating but did terrific work on your abs and core. Either way, it was something recruits hated, which is why it was a standard tool in the Company Commander's arsenal. These combined exercise sessions were known in recruit training as a Mash session, or "being mashed" as recruits call it.

As we began to approach the one-hour mark, White, Kozinski, and Jefferies were finished with their meals and was now nursing their drinks, no doubt nervous that if they finished their drinks, ultimately, they would have to join in the fun. But rest assured, that was not the plan

Daniels and I had in mind. Being this was in the dead of winter; the heat was on in the barracks, which made things pretty uncomfortable amid a Mash session. The heated barracks, combined with the fact that we had packed the compartment to twice its capacity, has brought the ambient temperature up to about 105 degrees and rising. I can't tell you what the humidity was, but I assure you it was extremely high. The recruits at this point were soaked from their own sweat, and the deck was just as wet from the same. The floors would get so wet; we had to be careful and ensure we switch to floor-based exercises once we got deep into a Mash session. Attempting to do jumping jacks, for instance, could cause injuries from slips and falls.

So, yes, while we were tough on the recruits, we also had the responsibility for their safety and well-being. Additionally, while we always pushed the recruits close to their physical limits, we had to ensure that our fellow Company Commanders and we never crossed over that proverbial line of physical abuse. From a recruit's perspective, it may appear that Company Commanders just didn't' care if someone got hurt or not, but in actuality, we cared very much.

After about 90 minutes had passed, it was so hot in the compartment, Daniels and I were also sweating, and all we were doing was giving orders. He walked over to the thermometer on the wall, looked back at me, and with a thumbs-up, proclaimed, "Yeah, baby, I think it's time!" The recruits were in the up push-up position. "Down!" I yelled out one final time. The recruits dropped to the floor in exhaustion. "Okay, listen up," I ordered. "I'm going to give you specific instructions that need to be followed to the letter. If they are not, you will mess up our surprise. If you mess this up, Chief Daniels and I will not be happy, and we will have to start this Mash session all over again. Do you understand? I asked loudly. "Yes, Sir!" came their loud and confident response in unison. "Okay, when I give the order, I want my company to get up and go to the windows and grab hold of the window handles. DO NOT open the windows until I say so. Understand?" I asked loudly to ensure confirmation. "Yes, Sir!" again came the response. "The rest of you," I continued, "will sit on the deck, legs crossed. Got it?" They agreed. As I gave the order to go, as instructed, the men quickly went to the exterior windows, placed their hands on the window handles, and waited for my orders. The rest of the men welcomingly sat up, crossed their legs, and relaxed, now realizing the punishment was over. They were all still breathing quite heavily, assuming and anticipating I was going to let in some cold air to cool them off. But they had no idea what was about to occur. I know this because it happened to me when I was in boot camp many years ago, and it's something I'll never forget.

I gave the command to open the windows on the count of three. "One, two, three!" I yelled, emphasizing the final number. Simultaneously, the recruits turn the window handles and pushed open the wing-type windows! The recruits were in awe as they began to realize what was happening. Because of the stark differences in the inside and outside temperatures, the cold air pouring in through the windows immediately turned into a fog. It began to roll down the outer bulkhead and across the floor, covering the deck entirely. It was a fantastic sight. I ordered the other recruits to sit on the floor as well.

The flog was about chest high, so all you could see was their head and shoulders above the cooling white cloud. I really can't describe the look on their faces. Some looked around in disbelief, while others smiled while enjoying the cooling effect it had on their bodies. But it wasn't over. Suddenly, the men began to hold out their hand's palm up, while looking towards the ceiling in confusion, as they began to feel what felt like cold raindrops. Well, that's precisely what was happening. Since heat rises, the hottest air in the compartment was resting at the ceiling level. Since the room was cooled down so quickly, condensation began to form on the ceiling; so much so, that drops of water began to fall on the men below, adding to an already amazing effect. So, on January 7th, 1989, on a cold winter afternoon, it literally rained indoors.

The Three Types of Ownership

There are so many valuable lessons that can be extracted from that story, aside from the fact that that with a little creativity (and about 170 sailors), you can actually bring fog and rain indoors. While the story was a bit longer than my usual, I felt it was necessary to share it with you, because it so powerfully demonstrates how critical the Ownership compartment of your Leadership vessel truly is. Additionally, it accurately sets the stage for the next lesson and shows how future leaders are encouraged and developed. Lastly, it instills, what I believe to be some of the most critical leadership elements within your Ownership compartment called the Three Types of Ownership. They are: Life Ownership, Team Ownership, and Executive Ownership

<u>1. Life Ownership – Taking Full Responsibility:</u> Seaman Recruit White, the Compartment Watch, didn't have to step forward and admit he left the lights on. He could have easily kept his mouth shut and no one would have ever known he was the one who caused a failed inspection. But instead, Seaman Recruit White took full responsibility. He knew he messed up, so he spoke up and owned the situation. That is Life Ownership and the making of a great future leader. Life Ownership simply means taking control of your life. It means owning everything that happens to you. A leader who possesses Life Ownership takes full responsibility for everything that happens to them. They live each day as if life is responding to them, not just happening to them. In summary, they don't blame others, regardless of the situation. In my last book, The Executive Arena, we discussed what I called victimhood, (the exact opposite of life ownership), and how it can affect your career and overall success. Well, it can also affect one's ability to lead.

You see, some get caught up in what I call The Blame Game, where nothing is their fault. "My boss was an asshole," "The Landlord wasn't fair," "It's because he lied to me," "They didn't give me enough time to complete the project," "The company doesn't care about their employees," "I know I'm always late, but traffic is horrible." Making excuses about why we failed at something, or why we aren't achieving the things we want, can quickly become a dangerous habit. Psychologists say that it's because we try to protect ourselves from anxiety and shame at a subconscious level. So, for example, when the question "why were you fired?" is asked, you will hear responses like, "I didn't get along with my boss" or "They didn't train me as promised." Rarely will you hear, "I was always late," or "I did a horrible job and didn't pull my own weight."

The problem is, the more we keep giving these unsubstantiated reasons or excuses (playing the blame game), the more we are impeding our ability to succeed, and effectively lead others. When the blame is continuously shifted away from ourselves, or our team, and towards someone or something else, we are programming our brain to believe: "I'm not in control, and there's nothing I can do next time to change the outcome." We go through life living in this victimhood mentality because, in a way, it makes us feel better about ourselves or our current situation. Unfortunately, while it may ease some anxiety and temporarily make us feel better, it does nothing to help us propel forward in our careers or to lead others.

The Leadership Arena

How do we rise above victimhood and put ourselves in complete control? There is only one way: Life Ownership! You must take 100% responsibility for everything that happens to you. And I mean everything! The relationship with your spouse or partner, the $10,000 in credit card debt, having to live paycheck to paycheck, even being in a job you hate. You must accept that it's all your fault. You must take 100% responsibility for your current situation and OWN IT if you are to gain control of it and make positive changes.

CRITICAL NOTE: "You must take personal responsibility. You cannot change the circumstances, the seasons, or the wind, but you can change yourself." -Jim Rohn

---

2. Team Ownership – Supporting the Weakest Link:

So why would we reward those three recruits who messed up with lunch from McDonald's? And believe me, during boot camp, McDonald's is a huge reward! Worse yet, why would we make them eat it in front of the other recruits who were getting mashed? You know, I've told this story dozens of times, and when I ask these very same questions, most seem to answer with some Hollywood version of what was going to happen next. I'll be the first to admit; the entertainment industry has done a pretty good job painting a picture of how "bad things" happen in boot camp. Stories of how the recruit who wouldn't shower, would suddenly find himself ambushed in the middle of the night and scrubbed with steel wool from head to toe. Or the guy who keeps failing inspection is blindfolded and beaten with sand-stuffed socks so you wouldn't see the bruises. I get a kick out of these stories because hey, it makes good television, right? However, while some of these stories may have been derived from some truth of many years ago, then, of course, embellished and retold with a new personality; in this case, nothing could be further from the truth. I assure you, if a Company Commander condones or even allows such behavior to occur today, he/she will find themselves in prison, or at the very least dishonorably discharged from the Navy. As I had mentioned before, there is a method to the madness.

In the case of Seaman Recruit White, let me start by saying he graduated as Seaman White, promoted to E-3 because he became the company's Honor Graduate. The company's vote awards this Honor Grad distinction. In other words, only recruits are allowed to vote for this award, and by the time they reached graduation, Seaman White was one of the best performing recruits in the company! How did this happen? You've heard the phrase; You're only as strong as your weakest link, correct? When it comes to teamwork, this statement is absolutely true, but where is the follow-up question? What do you do when you have a noticeable "weak link"? Answer: You make it stronger.

What you don't do is cut it off or remove the link. That's the last thing you want to do, but unfortunately, it's the first "go-to" for most inexperienced managers. Shortly after that special "raining indoors" day, two things happened. Firstly, Seaman Recruit White felt so bad that his fellow shipmates were being punished for his mistake, he made a vow then and there, to give 100% and do better! He was determined to make sure he did everything he could so as never to disappoint his team members again.

Secondly, the rest of the company absorbed the true meaning of the "weakest-link" phrase. They realized, for the company to be stronger, they had to make White stronger. So, from that point forward, many of White's shipmates began mentoring him. Some would help him study for upcoming academic exams, while others would coach him in military drill and inspections. This kind of team support, combined with White's determination to do better, laid the stage for the entire company to graduate with distinction.

Team Ownership means you support the weakest link and others who may need assistance. The ultimate goal is the success of the team, the company, the organization, not one's individual performance. Leaders who possess Team Ownership have constant thoughts of and live by the rule, 'together we rise' and it's a critical element in your leadership vessel.

By now, you should begin to realize that while each compartment of your leadership vessel is different, they are very much intertwined, each relying on the other for optimum performance. For instance, the recruits joined together to help Seaman Recruit White, an example of Team Ownership, but it was also a form of Mentorship. Additionally, the continued coaching and learning in itself is also a form of Studentship. From the Janitor to the Astronaut, from the secretary to the engineer, it takes everyone at NASA to launch that rocket successfully.

CRITICAL NOTE: "The strength of the team is each individual member. The strength of each member is the team." -Phil Jackson, NBA Champion, Coach and Executive.

---

3. Executive Ownership – Acting Like an Owner: How do I ensure my hard work gets noticed? This question is by far one of the most popular I get, whether during a coaching session or through the "Ask for Advice" option on Linked-In. While everyone's working situation is different, I always start by answering that question with a question: "If you became the owner of the company you currently work for, would you work any harder or differently than you do now?" To this day, I am still surprised by the answers I receive. Everything from the simple "Well, hell yeah I would!" to the more thoughtful "I would surely be thinking of new ways to improve our delivery process; it's not very productive right now." The

responses vary in content, but almost all of them answer, YES, I would work harder or differently. I also love seeing the lightbulb appear over their heads when they realize they just answered their own question.

As we discussed in my last book, being good at your job is only half the battle; there is so much more that goes into play when one is looking for that next promotion or raise. It's one of the main reasons I wrote The Executive Arena. Well, a part of that other 50% is what I call Executive Ownership.

Simply put, are you acting like an owner? You will hear many people say things like, "they don't pay me enough to do that," or "if they gave me a raise, I might stay late when needed." But that attitude is the very reason their "hard work" is not being noticed.

> CRITICAL NOTE: "People don't get promoted for doing their jobs really well. They get promoted by demonstrating their potential to do more!" -Tara Jaye Frank, www.BeLeaderly.com

Here are a few ways you can exhibit Executive Ownership at your place of employment regardless of your level or current position:

1. <u>Creative Thinking</u> – As the owner of a company, you would continuously be on the lookout for ways

to improve business. So, making recommendations to your superiors on how to improve a process perhaps, or how-to better capture customer satisfaction data is a good thing. Even if you present a couple of ideas that never get implemented, no one will hold that against you. In fact, this shows you are thinking about more than just your typical daily tasks. You are projecting the Perceptional Message™ (see The Executive Arena) that you are taking ownership, executive ownership, to be exact!

2. <u>First in, Last Out</u> – I can't stress enough about how important it is to show commitment to the business through managing your working hours. I'm not talking about putting in a bunch of overtime or working for free. What I'm saying is apply the <u>First in, Last Out</u> routine. Real leaders set the example, and there's no better way to do that then to be the first one in at the start of the day and the last one to leave. Imagine the perceptional message you are conveying when your boss notices you are always the first at work. Additionally, imagine the message and example you are setting for your subordinates if you are always the last to leave. Trust me; it makes a difference.

3. <u>Deliver more than expected</u> – Executive Ownership means doing more than what is expected. It means doing more than just completing a project a few days earlier than expected, though that can help. It means going above and beyond, performing outside of your job

description. For example, when I was working for a startup tech company back in Kansas City, Kansas, my wife and I came in on the weekend to assemble desk chairs and other office furniture. The company VP provided the pizza and drinks, and we spent the afternoon (with our 1-year old baby in a playpen) getting the location ready for its grand opening, though it was not required or expected. Delivering more than expected to a client, volunteering at a soup kitchen, stuffing gift bags for a company party, coming in after-hours to help paint an office are all examples of delivering more than expected.

As we bring this chapter to a close, you can clearly see how ownership is a vital compartment within your leadership vessel. Ownership, in all its forms, is not only an essential element of a great leader but also a mindset! It's how leaders think. From accepting full responsibility for your actions to supporting the weakest link. From putting the team first, to acting as if you own the place, ownership is an ingredient that strengthens the relationship between you and those you lead while improving the overall employer-employee relationship—just another one of those win-win situations.

LEADERSHIP LESSONS:

1. There are three types of Ownership: Life Ownership, Team Ownership, and Executive Ownership.
2. Life Ownership simply means taking control of your life. It means owning everything that happens to you. A leader who possesses Life Ownership takes full responsibility for everything that happens to them. They live each day as if life is responding to them, not just happening to them.
3. "You must take personal responsibility. You cannot change the circumstances, the seasons, or the wind, but you can change yourself." -Jim Rohn
4. Team Ownership means you support the weakest link and others who may need assistance. The ultimate goal is the success of the team, the company, the organization, not your individual performance.
5. Executive Ownership simply means acting like an owner. You can exhibit this quality through elements like creative thinking, "First-in, last-out" strategies, and delivering more than is expected.
6. With proper determination and motivation, (and about 170 sailors) you can make it rain indoors.

Chapter Eight: MANAGEMENTSHIP – Part One

Saturday, October 27th, 1990 – Guantanamo Bay Cuba

As I was finishing up my shift, sweeping off the fantail (rear) of the ship, I felt a tug on my left pant leg. I turned and looked down to find a little Haitian boy smiling back at me. He couldn't have been older than 4 or 5 years old, and the t-shirt he was wearing, dirty and stained, was obviously a men's large or something because it fit more like a dress as it hung well below the little boy's knees. From the big smile on his face, I highly doubt he realized the dangerous situation he was in, or where he was for that matter. To him, I'm guessing he was just hungry or thirsty after he and his family were rescued from his slowly deteriorating, wave-battered raft by the US Coast Guard two days ago. He was brought here to our ship, the USS Pensacola LSD-38, now docked at the US Naval Base, Guantanamo Bay Cuba, or "Gitmo" for short.

The Haitian refugee crisis that really began in late 1990 is what brought this little boy and me to meet on that warm sunny day in Cuba. The US Coast Guard was rescuing thousands of Haitian refugees from the rough waters of the Atlantic, then taking them to a refugee camp at Guantanamo Bay, Cuba. You see, many Haitians were fleeing by boat, raft, and whatever else would float after Jean-Bertrand Aristide, the democratically elected President of Haiti at the time, was overthrown, and the Cuban military government began persecuting his followers. They were extremely desperate because remaining in Haiti most surely meant they would be killed. So, their only hope at surviving was to stuff themselves and their families on a make-shift raft and start pedaling out to sea, literally.

The USS Pensacola, LSD-38 was a troop and equipment transport, sent to Gitmo to temporarily provide food, shelter and medical care for the rescued people of Haiti. The letters LSD didn't mean the ship was built in the 1960s during Woodstock. Okay, it was constructed in the 1960s, but the letters LSD stood for Landing Ship Dock. It was designed to carry LCAC's (Landing Craft Air Cushion), which were large hovercraft and other military equipment and troops. The rear of the ship would literally open up, allowing its entire Interior Well or bay to flood with seawater, so the LCAC's and other craft could quickly be launched and recovered. By leaving all the typical carried equipment back in Little Creek Virginia, this giant interior bay was filled instead with military cots, washbasins, make-shift showers, and clotheslines in support of the rescued.

The Leadership Arena

My shift was coming to an end, and today was especially exciting because the ship was planning a picnic for the entire crew. By picnic, I mean, live music, food, beer, all in an attempt to try and keep some sort of normalcy in the midst of this crisis. The word going around was we would be here through the holidays, but no one really knew for sure, so we just took it day by day, trying to remain optimistic that we'd at least be home by Christmas. Gitmo was hot, dry, dusty, and frankly not your typical Naval base. Amenities like stores, bars, gyms, etc. were very limited on the base, and what little they did have was reserved for those officially stationed at Gitmo, not for visiting vessels. We were to remain living on the ship, so believe me when I say this "picnic" was something everyone looked forward too.

I squatted down as best I could to get more eye-level with the little boy and smiled at him. With my forearms resting on my knees, I gave him a friendly greeting. "How's it going, little fella?" I asked, having no idea if he could understand me or not. At that moment, he reached out and was touching, no more-so, feeling my wristwatch. He seemed fascinated with the watch, which to me was some cheap Casio I picked up at the ship's store to use as a working watch. I think I paid like $20.00. "You like this watch?" I asked, again not sure if he understood. He smiled as he looked up at me, then back at the watch. "Tell you what," I said as I stood up and loosened the wristband, "You can have this to play with, okay?" When I removed the watch and placed it into his open hands, I was intrigued by this little guy's reaction. For a few seconds, he just stood there, the watch resting in his two hands, palms up, as if he were in awe at what had just happened. He slowly looked up at me with his eyes wide open, and a smile stretched across his face, which I interpreted as a sort of international thank you. "I think I made his day," I said to myself, and I quickly rubbed the top of his head, and went back to my sweeping. I smiled as I watch the now happy little boy run across the large well-deck, skipping every few steps, no doubt proud of his new gift, as he headed towards a large gathering of Haitian adults. Just moments later came the horrifying sounds I will never forget.

All the sailors currently on watch, including myself, heard the terrifying screams coming from what looked like a massive fight in the middle of the well-deck. With each passing second, more Haitians joined the ruckus, and a pile of kicking and yelling people began to grow in size. Just like the feeling you get during that first drop on a rollercoaster, my heart literally sank as the blood rushed to my head when I realized what was happening. The screams were coming from that little boy, as the adults from different families were almost tearing him apart, trying to get possession of the watch I gave him. I literally took a couple of steps back, not knowing what to do, almost frozen as I watched these savages pull and tear at this little boy over a cheap watch. Just then, a powerful stream of water hit the mound of people, almost immediately causing them to scatter. One of the sailors had turned on a firehose to break them up, and thankfully that did the trick. I didn't fully realize the gravity of the

The Leadership Arena

situation until a short time later, while getting changed for the ship's picnic, I was called to the Captain's office. That was the second time in a single day, my heart sank.

"Just wait here," said the Captain's messenger as he pointed to the bulkhead just to the left of the Captain's office door, "I'll let the Captain know you're ready." "You got it," I said as I turned to stand at parade rest, my back to the wall. The messenger knocked three times on the door, waited for the standard command of "enter" from the Captain, then went inside, closing the door slowly and softly behind him. I was a little concerned because the messenger had told me to come dressed as I am, which consisted of some swim trunks, sandals, and a t-shirt with the picture of a charging goat and the word's "Go Navy" printed in bold letters just below it.

Typically, being summoned to the Captain's office would require a dress uniform, but here I was ready to hit the beach and toss back a couple of beers, and my attire projecting that same message quite loudly. "I'm so screwed," I said quietly to myself. I couldn't help but ponder on the situation. I thought to myself, "by trying to do something nice for a little boy, I caused a dangerous situation that could have been a lot worse than it was if it wasn't for that firehose." Just then, the office door opened, and the Captain's messenger called me inside, "The Captain's ready for you now."

As I walked into the office, to my surprise, I immediately noticed Chief Roberts, my boss standing just to the side of the Captain's desk. The situation seemed to be getting worse with each passing minute. I walked over, stopped directly in front of the Captain's desk, and officially reported, "Sir, Petty Officer Spector, reporting as ordered, sir." "Have a seat Petty Officer," he said, "You too, Chief." We both looked at each other as the Chief, and I sat down in the two leather chairs facing the Captain. The Captain began. "I want to thank you both for taking the time to come see me. I know you'd both rather be out enjoying the festivities." "It's not a problem at all Sir," Chief Roberts answered. I remained quiet.

"Well, I'll make this quick and to the point," the Captain said. "As you both know, the situation that happened today in the well-deck was unfortunate. Thankfully no one was seriously hurt, and I wanted to let you both know that the little boy is fine. He had a little scratch on his arm, but that was the worst of it." "Thank you, Sir," I responded. "I also wanted to apologize to both of you," the Captain said very seriously. "Sir?" Chief Roberts questioned, not entirely understanding the Captain's remarks. "This was clearly a situation that could have been prevented, but the Chain of Command obviously broke down in this case, and that, starts with me. I should have been more transparent about our mission here at Gitmo, specifically, the mindset and sensitivity of the people we are dealing with." The Captain then turned to address me directly. "I understand why you did what you did. You were simply giving a gesture of kindness, and in the absence of any further information to say you shouldn't, you thought you were doing the right thing."

He then turned his attention to Chief Roberts. "Chief, we should have done a better job at preparing our men and instructing them on how and when to interact with our Haitian guests. My Officers and I should have been more transparent about what we are dealing with, and that's my fault." "I understand, Sir," chief Roberts replied.

"Now, I'm sure we have all learned that what may seem like a cheap watch to us, could be considered gold in the eyes of others, am I correct?" the Captain asked. In unison, we responded, "Yes, Sir!" "Good!" the Captain exclaimed. "I'll make sure we put together some sensitivity training and get it rolled out to all divisions ASAP. Let's make sure anyone assigned to caring for our guests has attended this training, so we don't have any further situations like this. Dismissed," the Captain ordered. We both nodded, stood up, and replied, "Yes, Sir!"

I followed Chief Roberts out of the office and gently closed the door behind us. "That was totally unexpected, and a great outcome," I expressed to Chief Roberts with a sigh of relief. "A great outcome?" he asked with a smile; no doubt also happy with the situation. "No, that's an example of a great leader," he concluded.

Managementship – Traits of a Great Boss

What is Managementship? To best answer that question, I need to refer you back to the chapter about What Leadership is NOT. If you recall, we talked about the fact that while all leaders are great managers, not all managers are great leaders. So, in this chapter, we are going to discuss those crucial traits that great managers possess.

Let's be honest, we all want to work for a great boss, and subsequently, we hope to be considered a great boss by others. So, what makes a great boss? When in a position of management, there is a right way and a wrong way to do things.

As leaders, we must also perfect the skills required to be a great manager. That specific skillset, and the sixth vital compartment in your leadership vessel, is called Managementship. Let's discuss those "great Boss" traits right now.

Transparency:

Aside from the story above being another perfect example of the importance of Ownership, (discussed in the previous chapter), it also teaches us the first essential element of Managementship; Transparency.

Being transparent simply means having open and honest communication between managers and employees. When we are honest with the people we manage about what's going on with the organization, it builds trust, and trust, as we all know now, builds loyalty. How many times have you experienced, let's say a massive layoff at an organization, but no one is really told why? In most cases, it comes as a surprise, and aside from a few senior management personnel and the HR department, everything is kept hush-hush until that "special day." Well, I'm not saying something like that should be announced, though there have been instances where companies did just that, I'm talking about after the fact.

Once the layoff is complete, once that location is shut down, or the division is dismantled, it's vital that we, as leaders, explain to those in our charge, why that business decision was made, and ensure they do the same with their people. It's not enough to just assume they understand the reasoning behind the choices we make as leaders. Even if they did, sitting down with your team and explaining what happened and why individual decisions were made, tells the employee "they are valued" as both a person and a valuable member of the team.

Another benefit of transparency is, it keeps everyone on the same page. As you saw from this last story, there was a breakdown in the chain of command, mostly due to a lack of transparency. Even though the Captain and perhaps some of his senior leadership may have known how sensitive the situation could be, that message can get lost as it's funneled down without consistent open and honest communication.

In an article from Glassdoor.com, titled The Benefits of Workplace Transparency, By Jessica Miller-Merrell in November of 2019, explains this significant "same page" concept. She writes, "It is never a bad idea to set expectations and make sure that everyone from senior leadership to managers down to frontline employees and so on, are on the same page. When the understanding of values, ethics, communication standards, plans, goals, etc. are the same from the bottom to the top, it doesn't leave a lot of room for misunderstanding. When one person is not aligned with the organization, it is significantly more likely that everyone below them will be out of line as well."

You see, this is precisely what happened with the story of the little boy and the Casio watch, only the Captain recognized the situation as a learning experience and corrected the transparency breakdown. Any less of a leader could have easily placed blame elsewhere, taking a "you should have known better" or "Don't let that happen again" attitude. Fortunately, he was a fantastic leader and an expert at Managementship.

After that whole ordeal with the little boy, I wish I could tell you that the story at Guantanamo Bay Cuba was over, but believe it or not, unbeknownst at the time, there were many more lessons to be learned that same day. I also wish I could tell you I didn't have to learn these upcoming lessons the hard way, but that wouldn't be open/honest communication now, would it?

Chapter Nine: MANAGEMENTSHIP - Part Two

Don't Bring Beer to The Batcave!

"Now that was kickass," Peterson commented as he boarded the shuttle, giving the driver a high-five as he passed, then taking a seat across the aisle from me. "I got some cool pictures of you, jumping off those rocks too," he added as he stretched his arms out across the back of the bench seat, settling in for the hot - dry trip back to the picnic area. This "shuttle," as we called it, was clearly an old school bus, now painted white with the words, United States Navy stenciled in black on each side of the bus. The lettering was only about 4" in height, so you really couldn't read it from a distance. I wasn't sure if that was by design, considering our location, or if it's just the largest they had available from their stencil library. Either way, it did the job. While some of the crew was still setting up things for our ship's picnic, a few of us decided to hit the beach and get some sun. Peterson was a fellow engineer from the boat, but we actually worked in different engine rooms. When he came aboard a year ago, we had become buddies when I was assigned to his indoctrination.

Because of the location of the naval base, there weren't many beaches per se, because of the rocky terrain. Most of the Cuban coastline we had access to on the base consisted of tall-rocky cliffs that stretched at least 15 to 20 feet high, which were mostly made up of jagged rocks and sharp coral. However, there was one area, literally in between the tall cliffs like it was cut out by the hand of God, where the sand was soft, white, and level, allowing direct access into the amazingly clear and warm salty waters. It was a small beach; I'm guessing a total of 150 feet of smooth coastline at a maximum, nestled inside this picturesque cove. The shuttle, every hour on the hour, would come to drop off and pick up sailors, all of whom were partaking in this little secret patch of paradise.

The air-conditioning on the bus consisted of having all the windows down and keeping our speed of travel above 35 mph when possible. This minimum speed kept some sort of hot breeze moving through the compartment while preventing the dust that was being kicked up from the dry dirt road behind us, from entering through the windows and sticking to our already sweaty bodies. Even though the bus was hot, and the picnic area was just a half-mile down the road, the shuttle was still a much better choice than walking in the scorching sun, having to deal with the choking dust you'd be hit with every time a vehicle passed.

Peterson and I had had our little taste of paradise and was heading back to the picnic to grab some food and enjoy the party. This event was a very welcomed moment since

The Leadership Arena

most of us were constantly reminded that we could be here stuck here in Gitmo through the holidays and for the foreseeable future. Again, no one really knew for sure.

As the bus pulled into the gravel-lined designated parking area, Peterson grabbed his towel and headed for the door. As soon as the driver cut the engine, I could faintly hear what sounded like steel drums and a bass guitar piercing the air as we all got up to exit the bus. "Let's go, man, there's a cold beer calling us. I can hear it!" Peterson exclaimed. "No argument there," I said.

It was perfect! The area chosen for this picnic was absolutely beautiful. It was full of shade trees, and the grass-covered grounds was a welcomed change from the usual sand and dirt. It was located right on the water, but we weren't actually at sea level. Peterson and I both plunged our arms, elbow deep into a huge barrel of ice water, each pulling out a cold beer as we passed one of many beverage stations without missing a step. We were walking into the breeze coming off the ocean, moving towards the coast to get a better view of the water and a clearer understanding of where we were.

As we approached the edge of the grass, we stopped, looked at each other, smiled, and tapped our cans together. "Cheers," he said as we both looked out towards the ocean to take in the view. We were not standing on a beach; we were standing on the edge of a small cliff. I looked over the edge to notice a long stretch of very weathered wooden stairs that lead down to the turbulent waters below. I'm guessing it was about 40 feet down to the sea, and the stairs resembled the construction of an old inner-city fire escape. It zig-zagged its way down the rocky cliffside, perhaps providing access to the water below for those who wanted to do some snorkeling. At least that was my guess derived from the faded wooden sign nailed to the handrail that read, 'Snorkeling Access.'

"Okay," Peterson began as he crushed his now empty beer can between the palms of his hands, "now that I've had a beer, it's time to eat." I chuckled then quickly finished off my beer as we both headed towards the two large charcoal grills, smoking with enticement. "Let's grab one more beer first," Peterson suggested, making a quick turn towards another ice-filled barrel, "As I've always said," he joked, "I can't eat on an empty stomach."

For the next hour, we simply just enjoyed all this afternoon had to offer. Live music, hotdogs, burgers, corn on the cob grilled in the husks, even potato salad brought over from the ship's galley, made this a real Kodak moment. For a minute, I began to think about the little boy I met earlier that day, and the commotion I caused over a single gesture of kindness. I smiled to myself, shook my head, took another drink of my beer, and just settled in gratefulness (and into my beach chair) that nothing more serious had come from my oversight. All in all, it was a good day. Well, it was a good day until we heard the words, "Hey, you guys want to hit the surf?"

The Leadership Arena

That question came from Petty Officer Roy and Sidekick as they came around from our backside caring flippers, mask, and snorkel, and an orange uninflated CO2 charged vest in their hands. "You can get all the equipment you need, for the entire day for free, right over there," said Roy as he pointed to a large brown tent, set up about 20 yards away. "Well, it will cost you $5.00 if you inflate the vest, a little charge for the CO2 cartridge when you return the equipment, but it's still a great deal, and I don't foresee inflating the vest.". Roy, and Sidekick, whose name still escapes me to this day, were Navy Divers assigned to our ship for this deployment at Gitmo.

Roy used to be an active Navy Seal early in his career and had recently decided to finish out the last few years before his retirement as a Navy Diver. From what I had understood, it wasn't uncommon for Seal Team members to become instructors or salvage and rescue divers as they got up in age. We had met Roy and said Sidekick at the enlisted club on base a couple of weeks before, and we all hit it off. We were sort of "shore buddies" I guess you can call it. We never saw each other while working on the ship, though we would hang out after work onboard, or party together when the opportunity presented itself onshore.

"I'm game if you are!" Peterson injected. "Oh, what the hell," I agreed, "It's getting pretty hot just sitting here anyway." We both got up from our comfy beach chairs and followed Roy and his partner towards the little brown tent. "Hey, since we just ate, aren't we supposed to wait an hour before we swim?" Peterson snickered. "Only if you're in the Army," Roy concluded. "He's right," I agreed in a serious tone, "Army guys can't function with a tummy ache."

Within ten minutes, we all had our snorkeling gear and had begun our barefoot descent down the cliffside, being careful not to get a splinter from the weathered wooden stairs. The only smart ones were Roy and Sidekick who not only had brought their own professional mask and fins, Roy correctly was wearing a pair of diving slippers as they are called. These were slippered-type shoes made of thick rubber that you tightly pulled over your feet, and most times, a requirement for strap on fins. Roy and Sidekick were moving the quickest down the steps towards the water, followed by myself pushing a little slower. In last place was Peterson, who was comically attempting the navigate the steps wearing his flippers! You couldn't help but laugh.

At the bottom of the steps was a square wooden landing, approximately 6-feet in length that rested a few inches below the water. Again, this was not a beach and the sea, the best we could tell was approximately 30 feet deep at the landing. It was difficult to know precisely because the water was so clear that it appeared to be only a couple of feet deep at the most. As the ocean ebbed and flowed, waves would breach the wooded landing hitting the rocky cliff behind us before reversing and going back out to sea. While you were putting on your equipment, you couldn't set anything down, or within seconds the waves could carry it out to sea. Just to put on my fins, I had to hold my mask and snorkel in my teeth, with one fin held tightly under my left arm, while putting on the other. It felt very clumsy, and Peterson's laughable approach to wear his fins down the stairs, was beginning to look like that would have the more sensible thing to do. "Had he done this before?" I thought to myself.

One at a time, we each entered the somewhat rough water by jumping as far as we could out and away from the cliffside, then quickly swimming a few yards away from the wooden landing. By merely stepping off the dock, you risked being slammed up against it, or the sharp rock and coral lined cliffside by the incoming waves. We each made it safely into the water, and the further we swam away from the shoreline, the calmer the ocean seemed to become. At about 50 yards out, the once turbulent environment had transformed into a tranquil tropical paradise. With our masks in place and snorkels at the ready, we gave a final nod as we lowered our faces into the Cuban waters. The once verbal communication was now nothing more than eye contact, head, and hand gestures.

This being my first time snorkeling in any real waters, it felt like you were in a whole new world, almost like a dream. The most brilliant colored schools of fish would pass you by like you weren't even there. A couple of giant stingrays glided along the bottom of the sandy ocean floor, paying no attention to the four of us invading their domain for some entertainment. Other large fish came so close I could literally touch them, (and a couple I did) as if they were almost welcoming me somehow. It was at that moment I realized that I was in their world now. We were visitors.

After about 10 minutes, Peterson singled for us to surface, which we all did. "Hey, Peterson began, "why don't we head down to that beach we were at this morning?" "You mean that little cove the guys were shuttling to all day?" Roy asked. "Yeah, it can't be far, and we just follow the coastline straight west and catch the shuttle back," Peterson suggested. We all agreed, as we donned our masks and entered to water heading due west.

For the next 45 minutes or so, we continued to enjoy the fantastic, slow-moving world of beauty below us as we continued to make our way along the coastline. Each of us would take turns every couple of minutes to surface, regularly on the lookout for our destination. But the destination never came. In fact, we never even saw any kind of clearing or break in the cliff-like coastline where we could safely swim ashore. Just as when we first entered the water, the shoreline was precisely as it was then – Tall cliffs of sharp rock and coral at least 20 to 30 feet high, where the sea became more turbulent the closer you got to land. As the others surfaced, I could feel we were all a little worried about where the hell that small cove was located. "Did we pass it?" Peterson asked. "No way," Roy said confidently, "I've been watching for it." I turned to look east, back in the direction we had come and said, "Well, we can't go back; I have no idea how far we have come." "Well, the cove can't be too much further," Sidekick injected, "so I suggest we find a place to rest for a few minutes, then continue on towards the cove." "You mean like that cave over there?" Peterson said, even surprising himself that he found something as he pointed towards a large opening in the cliffside. "Let's do it!" I said, "We could use a break."

There was a sense of relief as we all swam toward the large opening, now realizing that we were going to be able to rest for a while. But as we drew closer to the cave, it became evident the large opening was not as big as we had initially assumed, at least not big enough for all of us to swim through at the same time. Furthermore, as waves rolled in, they would smack the top of the cave opening so we would have to time our entrance to the cave to match the wave patterns. Roy, who was clearly the most experienced swimmer, was the first to go.

We all watched, hoping to repeat what he did precisely if he was successful, of course. Roy swam over and positioned himself directly in front of the cave. A wave rolled in, slightly lifting Roy up, then back down as it passed him, then crashing against the top of the rocky cave opening. As soon as the water retreated, exposing the now wide cave opening, Roy quickly swam straight towards the entrance. The next wave to roll in actually helped push him into the cave. "This is perfect!" Roy yelled out from inside the cave. "The air is cool in here; come on in!" Sidekick was next, then Peterson both following how Roy safely entered the cave. I was last, and for a second, I thought I heard a voice saying, "Great, if someone's going to get hurt, it's going to be the last guy." Thankfully, that voice was wrong - this time.

Inside, the cave was much lighter than any of us expected, considering the only source of light was the entrance we just swam through. It was filled with these ledges we could sit on, which looked like smooth river rocks, only these rocks were about the size of a Volkswagen. They were perfectly rounded and as smooth as glass, no doubt formed after years of saltwater, and sand, polishing each stone a little more with every passing wave. I pulled myself out of the water onto an almost entirely flat rock. For the first time in about an hour, I was able to sit completely relaxed, with my feet hanging off the edge, and soaking in the rushing waters.

The air was cold, and the soothing sounds of the ocean waves, now echoing off the cave walls was almost therapeutic. I doubt many other sailors have found this place, or at least that was my guess. Either way, it was a pretty special place and another one of those navy moments you don't soon forget. Nor what was about to happen next.

Just then, Peterson spoke the last thing I would ever expect to hear in a situation like this. "Who wants a beer?" he called out. At first, I laughed, thinking he was just making light of our situation until I noticed him putting his hands down his swim trunks, pulling out a can of beer.

One, two, three, then the fourth can of beer was pulled from his shorts and placed on the rock next to him. I could not believe my eyes. Somehow, Peterson had managed to store four cans of beer in the interior netted pockets of his swim trunks. "They're a little warm from the water, but it's better than nothing," he said as he grabbed a can and held it up. Who in the hell would even think of bringing beer while snorkeling? Worse yet, what kind of person would also want a beer at a time like this? "I'll take one!" I yelled as I raised both my hands, signaling that I was ready to catch one. He tossed me the first can, then another to Sidekick. Roy declined while stating we "weren't normal" and suggested if we made it back alive, we should check in with Sickbay (the Medical Clinic) as soon as possible. "That just means two for the carrier," Peterson said as he cracked open his can and chugged about half of it down.

As we sat enjoying our much-earned beverage, there was a lull in wave activity, and for a few seconds, it became very quiet. So much so, that we heard a kind of rustling noise coming from the dark cave ceiling above us. "Holy shit!" Sidekick exclaimed in a panicking whisper. "They're Bats! Hundreds of them". I immediately looked up, and as my eyes slowly adjusted to the darkness above, I could finally see the entire roof of the cave literally lined with bats. "Wow, we found the Bat Cave!" yelled Peterson. "Keep your voice down," I demanded, "You don't want to startle them." It was then that I realized our little hidden paradise was not so exclusive or therapeutic any longer. "Startle?" Peterson asked as he held up the last can of unopened beer with a shit-eaten grin that stretched from ear to ear. "Don't, you, dare!" Roy threatened slowly and firmly as he pointed directly at Peterson. With a smile, and in what looked like slow-motion, Peterson, with an underhand toss, launched that single can of beer towards the cave ceiling.

As soon as the can of beer left his fingertips, the hundreds of bats, sensing the incoming danger, almost simultaneously took flight. There we so many, in such close proximity, I could hardly see and could literally feel the breeze created from their wings blowing across my face and body. I immediately jumped into the water, attempting to get myself as low as possible, away from the now startled and frantically flying bats. I quickly realized the others followed my thought process and had jumped in the water, now heading towards the cave exit. Once again, we had to time our departure with the rhythm of the waves, only this time with bats clouding our concentration. Somehow, we all made it out of the cave safely, but now, thanks to Peterson, we were truly exhausted, and the cove we were searching for was still nowhere in sight.

I knew the situation was getting serious when Roy and Sidekick both pulled the emergency cords hanging from their shoulder, activating the CO_2 cartridge and inflating their life vests. Peterson and I both followed suit after

The Leadership Arena

Roy announced his reasoning for pulling the cord, "Hey, I may be good swimmer, but I'm not stupid; I'll pay the 5-bucks!" As the four of us bobbed up and down in the water, hugging our now inflated life vests, we quickly discussed our options. We could one, head back to the point from which we came; two, keep swimming west along the coast searching for the cove; or three, attempt to scale the 20-30-foot rocky cliffside to get ashore. We all agreed to option three. Going back or swimming forward were both uncertainties as neither of us was sure of our exact location. Additionally, continuing to swim would only drain more energy, eventually forcing us to attempt a climb out regardless. We all agreed, scaling the rocky cliff was worth the risk and put together a plan.

We would find the best section to climb and situate ourselves on the jagged rocks below. Roy would go first since he had the diving slippers. We would hold his equipment, (including his fins because you can't climb a cliff with huge flippers on your feet), while he scaled the cliffside. Once he safely reached the top, we would toss up his equipment to him, and he would throw down the slippers for the next person to use. Without the slippers, you would easily cut up your feet, or worse slip on the rock and coral-filled cliffside, risking severe injury. I couldn't help but think of those climbing walls you see at shopping malls or on cruise ships, only this one didn't come with a safety harness or rubber mats to break your fall. Nor did it come equipped with strategically placed handles to grab and help navigate your way to the top. That little voice once again began speaking saying, "If someone is going to get hurt today, this is where it's going to happen."

Roy reached the top of the cliff reasonably quick, and as discussed, immediately tossed down the slippers to Sidekick, who ascended the wall just as fast. Peterson did pretty well but needed a little help from the guys when he reached the top to pull him up and over the edge. With a smile, Peterson dropped the slippers to me announcing, "It's all you baby!" I looked up to see all three gazing over the edge, ready to assist once I got near the top.

I donned the diving slippers and began my climb. It wasn't as tricky as I had anticipated, and watching how the other three maneuvered up the cliff before me, was undoubtedly beneficial. Just as they did with Peterson, as soon as my hands reached the top, Roy and Sidekick both grabbed an arm and pulled me up and over to safety. I swear as I sat down on the now grassy ground, I think I actually heard the four of us in unison, let out a sigh of relief. We made it.

After about a minute or two of rest and observing our surroundings, taking note of the light forest directly to our south, we decided we would head through the trees to find a main road or path back to familiar ground. We each picked up our gear, Roy slapped Peterson in the back of the head for the whole beer and bat fiasco, then we headed into the trees.

It wasn't more than five minutes before I called out, "Everyone Stop, Listen!" We all stopped in our tracks, and I looked over at Roy, who was leading the way. Roy turned around, looked at me in disbelief, and said, "That can't be what I think it is, Right?" I shrugged my shoulders in response, and Roy turned to head directly east towards the sound we now all heard clearly. We walked much quicker now in a single file line towards the sound of steel drums and a bass guitar. As the music increased in volume, it was suddenly accompanied by the smell of burning charcoal and grilled meats, and we began to hear muffled human voices in a conversation. As each one of us exited the edge of the forest, stepping into the familiar clearing, we stopped and stared while our brains struggled to comprehend how this could be? Here we were, right back at the picnic area, we had left almost two hours ago. How could we have traveled so far in the water, only to find out we were only about 200 yards away from our starting point by land? It wasn't until we returned our equipment, paid the now owed $5.00 CO_2 charge, and talked to the locals that we realized what had transpired.

Plotting Your Course and Navigating the Waters!

When we first entered the water and began to travel west in search of the cove we had visited before, we were unaware of the water conditions, nor were we sure where that hidden cove was located. You see, on this side of the island, the current was powerful and tracked east, opposite the direction we were trying to swim. While we thought we were swimming a considerable distance along the coast, in actuality, we had only traveled just far enough away from our starting point, to where the wooden staircase and dock was no longer in view. With the entire shoreline looking pretty much exactly the same, there were no landmarks to help track our progress. This east-moving coastal current was also the reason the water along the cliffside was so turbulent, and the reason we grew tired more quickly than one usually would. We were literally experiencing that famous phrase "swimming against the tide." Let's discuss the remaining elements of effective managementship and how you can ensure your team sails towards success!

> CRITICAL NOTE: If you don't plot your course and take the time to study the waters you will be sailing, you may soon find yourself adrift, your direction at the mercy of your circumstances.

Having Direction: One of the essential elements of effective managementship is having direction! When Peterson and I jumped in with both feet into unknown waters, only having an "idea" of where we were going, we were doomed to fail. As a leader, you are the Captain of your leadership vessel, and as such, you must be confident in where you are going and how to get there. In any branch of the military, having a clear direction and the confidence you will achieve your mission is Managementship-101. Simply put, if you don't believe you will succeed, the people you lead won't either. In other words, the Platoon Sergeant knows, beyond any doubt, they will take that hill. The Captain of a ship knows they will defend that island, and the Sales Manager knows his team will break the company sales record. Exuding this kind of confidence combined with preparedness, is in large part, the fuel that motivates your team.

When you are not sure of yourself or your direction, haphazardly trying to "make it through another day" causes many to fall into a reactive vs. proactive work pattern. You'll spend most of your energy putting out fires, instead of focusing on and sailing towards your final destination. The lesson here is this: Your people must believe in you, or you just may find yourself stranded on a rock in a bat cave, pulling warm beers from your shorts. And please trust me when I say, it's not a pretty picture.

Plot Your Course:

If you are not sure which path to take or keep changing direction because the seas get a little rough, your people won't follow. It's one thing to have guidance, to know what you want to achieve, and clearly convey that to your team. However, you must plot the course. Long before a ship ever sets sail, you must plan your route with waypoints. Waypoints are specific points during a journey, at which time something happens. For instance, we will travel north for 28 miles at full speed to the first waypoint, at which time we will turn due east and slow to standard speed. In other words, the best way to describe "plotting your course" is to have a plan!

Believe it or not, 80% of all new businesses fail within the first year! Yes, you read that correctly. Eight out of every ten new companies fail before they've even hit 12 months in operation. Of those that do survive past 12 months, 50% of those will never make it to the five-year mark. If you do your research on why this statistic is so high, you will see many reasons, from lack of capital to not being prepared for sudden growth, to failing to market properly online, among many others. But all these specific reasons point to one big issue and another crucial element in managementship: Plotting your course!

There's an old saying that says, "If you fail to plan, you are planning to fail." This statement still holds true today, but it applies to so much more than just business plans for new start-ups. It applies to you and the way you manage your people as well. For example, when you treat your department or division as a new business and create a plan to achieve your department goals, your chances of success go up drastically. The best example of plotting the course within a department is when we manage the sales department's metrics.

I'll be the first to admit, when I was a salesperson very early in my corporate career, I hated having to "go over the numbers" with my manager. However, time and time again, going over these metrics proved extremely beneficial. My manager was providing not only a clear direction; he was plotting the course. For example, I knew in order to make one sale; I had to meet with three people face to face. To comply with three people, face to face, I had to set at least six appointments, because I knew only about 50% would actually show up for the meeting. This managed statistic was called the "show rate." Lastly, just to set a single appointment, I had to make at least 20 phone calls. So, knowing all these facts (Metrics), it was easy to plot my course for the day. My goal was clear; I had to make 120 phone calls a day to ensure I made at least one sale. Most importantly, knowing all these "waypoints" made it easy to check my progress to ensure I was on course, and to make adjustments when needed.

In an article from Successharbor.com by editor and co-founder George Meszaros titled, "50 Reasons Why Some Business Fail and Others Succeed", number two at the top of the list was Leadership Failure. It reads, "Businesses fail because of poor leadership. The leadership must be able to make the right decisions most of the time. From financial management to employee management, leadership failures will trickle down to every aspect of your business. The most successful entrepreneurs learn, study, and reach out to mentors to improve their leadership skills." Are you beginning to see a pattern here?

Regardless of your current leadership level at your organization, as a leader, it's your job to plot the course for your company, division, department, or even your small sales team as well as the individuals of which whom are a part of that team. Don't leave this planning up to your organization. They hired you to do a job and to lead them to success, so LEAD! Lastly, this not only applies to individual job functions or department goals; but each individual's personal and professional development or studentship (as discussed in an earlier chapter) can all be plotted and navigated.

One final lesson on plotting your course before moving on: In business and in life, rarely does everything go as planned. Things will come up that can throw us off course, it's inevitable. Companies restructure, employees unexpectedly quit, mistakes are made, and yes, even bad decisions can all knock us off course. But you can't get your leadership vessel back on track unless you've plotted and set that course in the first place.

Other Managementship Elements

Taking Calculated Risks: The best things in life are resting just outside your comfort zone. Let that statement sink in for a bit. Everything you have ever wanted, the best things in life that you have dreamed about for a while now, are just sitting there waiting for you right outside your comfort zone. All you have to do is go for it by allowing yourself to enter uncomfortable situations. It's called taking calculated risks.

The most successful leaders you will ever meet are, in large part, risk-takers. To them, taking calculated risks are just a part of life and a necessary ingredient on the road to greater success. These risks, not to be confused with gambling, like playing the horses, or buying lottery tickets, can come in all shapes and sizes. For example, leaving a stable job of 10 years to take a position with a start-up company that has a promising future, or accepting that new position that will require you to relocate your entire family across the country, are all examples of taking risks! However, it's not very easy to do because of how we, as humans, are wired.

You see, it's human nature to want to be and remain comfortable. For example, if you've ever been to a moving theater, and I'm speaking about the older ones, where the seats were never very cozy, those theaters were designed to pack as many people in as possible. Much like the commercial airplane of today, the seats were NOT designed for comfort. Anyway, we will sit and watch the movie, not moving until all of a sudden, one of our butt cheeks start to go numb. What did you do? You would move or shift in your seat until you once again were "more comfortable." If you are an experienced traveler, you have also experienced these butt-numbing situations many times over.

The point here is that the vast majority of people want to remain in a state of comfort, only getting off their butt (no pun intended) and doing something when they become uncomfortable. However, their goal, when they do finally do something, is to get back to that state of comfort, where they feel safe. It's an entirely different mindset vs. the mindset of successful leaders. But don't just take my word for it, science has proved the same point.

Sam Roberts, CEO of VUDU Marketing and Author of Screw the Zoo, wrote an article for Entrepreneur.com Titled, Here's What Science Says You Should do to Achieve Greater Success. In this article, Sam writes, "Everyone wants to be more successful, even though definitions of success vary wildly. You might picture success as accumulating wealth, or as achieving a position of power in an organization, or even as having more time to spend with your family members and friends. Strangely enough, there's one pattern of thinking that's important to achieving <u>any</u> measure of success, no matter how you define it... Being comfortable taking risks." I love the way Sam put it in his subtitle when he said, "Taking risks may seem scary, but risk is the moat standing between you and true success."

Look, I didn't invent this concept as it's been a proven trait of the hugely successful since the beginning of time. All the greats have taught and continue to show the same thing in their own special and unique way.

- <u>Mark Zuckerberg</u>: "The only strategy that is guaranteed to fail is not taking risks."
- <u>Jack Canfield</u>: "Everything you want is on the other side of fear."

The Leadership Arena

- Jim Rohn: "If you're not willing to risk the unusual, you will have to settle for the ordinary."
- Richard Branson: "You can't run a business without taking risks. The Brave may not live forever – but the cautious don't live at all!"
- Brian Tracy: "Move out of your comfort zone. You can only grow if you are willing to feel awkward and uncomfortable when you try something new."
- Robert Kiyosaki: In today's rapidly changing world, the people who are not taking risks are the risk-takers."

As I have already said, "The best things in life are waiting for you just outside your comfort zone." So, get uncomfortable! Start that new business, accept that new position located 1000 miles away, spend 12 months writing that book, accept that promotion in which you feel unprepared or under-skilled, because the alternative is mediocrity at best.

Perhaps we should look at it this way: If we take a risk in something we believe in, do we ever really fail? We took a chance (a silly one) when we decided to jump into those Cuban waters and attempt to swim over a half-mile in search of some little piece of paradise. In that example, we failed to reach our destination, but that's okay because we learned some valuable lessons from that experience.

> CRITICAL NOTE: Rest assured, when you take risks, there will be successes and there will be failures. But those failures come with increased knowledge because you can learn something valuable from every experience. This gained knowledge in itself becomes a success.

Making Decisions and Making Mistakes: "If you're not making any mistakes, you're not making enough decisions." This statement was a brilliant piece of wisdom that was passed on to me many years ago. This advice came from the President of a tech company I worked for back in Chicago. Let's call him Ken.

As it relates to managementship or even business as a whole, one would think the goal is to make as few mistakes as possible, right? I mean, no one purposely tracks their mistakes, having some number listed on a spreadsheet labeled daily metrics. Generally, we go about our day completing the tasks required of us, consciously trying to avoid any mistakes, if at all possible. This is how the vast majority of us think, and we've all been taught, the fewer mistakes, the better. However, Ken's approach to business success was a bit different in regard to making decisions and making mistakes. And it's something that has stuck with me throughout my entire career.

You see, I combined these two topics Making Decisions and Making Mistakes into one section because they belong together. Like the Yin and Yang symbol, both sides of this black and white symbol need to be equally balanced for either side to flourish. In fact, they need each other, which is why there is the opposite color's dot on each opposing side of the Yin Yang symbol. In other words, it takes balance to bring wholeness.

> CRITICAL NOTE: You can't nurture creativity and make significant decisions that grow your department or organization if you are too afraid of making mistakes!

Sometimes we find ourselves searching for or waiting for "more information" much too long before deciding between Plan-A or plan-B because we are so afraid of choosing the wrong path. This indecision, in turn, leads to bad decisions, which is precisely what we don't want. In the business world, some professionals call it analysis paralysis. We get so caught up in trying to be right, that we lose sight of the finish line.

Not to sound too much like a karate sensei, there are three questions I ask myself that have always seemed to bring a sense of balance to any stringent decision-making process:

1. What will the impact of my decision be on the department, division, or company if I'm right?
2. What will the impact of my decision be on the department, division, or company if I'm wrong?

3. If I'm wrong, how quickly can I reverse the decision or change course to correct my mistake?

Once you know the answer to those three questions, particularly the last one, you should be prepared to make a sound decision. Additionally, having the answers to all three questions above ensures you will learn from your mistake, should your choice turn out to be the wrong one.

Lastly, just as Ken shared this advice with me, so should you share this advice with those in your charge. Instill in the people you lead that it's okay to make mistakes, because this, in turn, seeds creativity and decisiveness in tomorrow's leaders. In summary, throughout our careers, we will make mistakes, and that's okay, as long as we learn and grow from them.

<u>Roll Up Your Sleeves and Delegate:</u>
Concerning becoming a great boss, two other Yin and Yang elements of Managementship that go together are Rolling Up Your Sleeves, meaning jumping in and doing the work yourself, and Delegating, or assigning specific tasks or responsibility to others. At first glance, these two elements may seem counterproductive, but once again, like making decisions and making mistakes, there must be a happy balance between both to ensure growth.

Let's start with the rolling up your sleeves element of being a great boss. I'm sure you have heard during job interviews, or seen many times in job postings, the phrase "looking for someone to roll up their sleeves and get the job done." It's almost become commonplace, but unfortunately, a lot of times, the phrase is both misused and misunderstood. Take, for example, a posting for a VP of Sales position that reads, "Looking for a go-getter who will roll up their sleeves and bring in new business for our growing company." Now, in this example, the organization may have genuinely been looking to fill a senior management position. However, a top management candidate seeking a VP role could read this and think, "That's not a real VP role; it's merely a sales position with a VP title," and never send in his/her resume. Now, I'm not going to get into how to write job postings correctly or how to attract the right talent, that's for another book entirely. The point here is great leaders are not afraid or too proud to roll up their sleeves, jump in, and help out when necessary. Managementship, in part, means managing the resources you have, including yourself when need be, to achieve the organization's goals.

Additionally, some managers get confused about the whole "rolling up your sleeves" thing, believing, unfortunately, in the exact opposite of delegating. In other words, some have the mindset of "if you want something done right, you have to do it yourself." They horde entire projects, never delegating any part to others, sometimes to the point of missing deadlines, because they just can't let go. They don't trust their employees to do the work correctly, and thus their employees don't trust them in return. Without delegation, there is no trust, without trust, there is no loyalty, and without loyalty, you're swimming against the tide.

Rolling up your sleeves, and delegation are the Yin and Yang of employee trust and can effectively coexist simultaneously. When you delegate challenging and essential tasks to your subordinates, you are not only confirming that you trust them but also helping them grow by teaching them new skills. In return, they become more confident in their abilities, increasing their knowledge and overall performance for the organization, thus increasing Human Capital.

To be brutally honest, the ineffective manager arrogantly feels they are the best person in the room, and never delegates. A great leader in perfect balance will delegate important tasks while standing by, ready and willing to roll up their sleeves and jump in to <u>assist</u> (not take over), if and when the need arises. It's like saying, "I'm here to help; let's do this together." It's just another example of authentic leadership being about setting the stage for others' success, assisting when needed, and allowing their team to take the spotlight. But to do that, you must be both willing to help and willing to delegate. Like teaching a child to ride a bike, you know they're going to fall and get some scratches along the way, but they will never learn unless you're willing to point them in the right direction, give them a push, and let go!

Working From Home is So "Old School"

The Leadership Arena

As we bring this chapter to a close, there is one final element, and perhaps one of the most important as it pertains to Managementship and being a good boss. Throughout this book thus far, we have discussed the element of trust numerous times in multiple chapters. Regardless of what compartment we are constructing aboard our leadership vessel, trust seems to be a significant ingredient like the navy gray-colored paint used throughout all navy ships. This in itself proves the significance of how trust, or lack thereof, can make or break you as a leader. So, hold that thought for a moment and let me set this up.

> CRITICAL NOTE: No matter how hard you try, no matter your level of experience, you cannot be an effective leader without TRUST.

Many years ago, I was afforded the luxury of a home office. The company provided me with a desktop computer, satellite access to the internet, a fax machine, a separate phone line (hardwired), and a flip-phone (ancient cell phone) that had great reception if I pulled out the little plastic antenna and went outside. Twenty years ago, this kind of set up was at great expense to a company, only afforded in large part, to the most senior of executives, or sometimes if your job description included a term known as Road Warrior. Today, however, our advances in technology from amazing smartphones to videoconferencing, to inexpensive tablets and laptops, most of which are more powerful than a company's central server of 20 years ago, make it much easier to work remotely. Oh, and by the way, we need to stop using the term "working from home" because that's so old school. Today we can work from a beach chair with an iPhone in one hand and a margarita in the other, just as efficiently as we can from our office desk. The term should be Working Remotely.

The point is, the expense or difficulty in setup, is no longer a factor when it comes to allowing someone to work remotely. There is really no excuse, not too. It doesn't cost the company any more to allow certain employees to work remotely; in a lot of cases, it could actually save the company money. So, knowing this basic information, why do organizations still have such a hard time with the concept of working remotely? You guessed it; Trust.

It's sad to say, but the majority of management personnel in today's workforce just don't trust their employees. It's true! How many of you have heard about or have directly worked for a boss that was a stickler for how many hours one works in a single day? Or how about the manager that frowns at any person who leaves right at 5 PM, even though that's the official end of the workday? Or, even worse, how about times when an employee calls in sick, and the manager immediately assumes said employee is "probably interviewing for another job"? In all these situations, there is a significant lack of trust. This lack of

The Leadership Arena

trust is why it's so difficult for some managers to accept the concept of working remotely.

Now, don't confuse these situations with a manager who is dealing with an employee who is consistently late, or has excessive absences; that's an entirely different arena. I'm talking about the manager who's a "clock Watcher." Perhaps you are one of those managers reading this book right now. If so, you may be asking yourself, "If I allow people to work remotely, how will I know they are putting in a full day's work?" Well, aside from the fact that I have an issue with the phrase "full day's work," let me simply answer your question, with a question - <u>Are they getting the job done?</u> It's that simple. Are they successfully doing the job you hired them to do? If they are, then what are you worried about? If they are doing the job and doing it well, do you really care if they did it in six hours or eight?

This isn't the industrial age anymore, where employee success was widely graded by the number of hours one worked in a day or the number of years someone was employed at a single company. We want great employees, yet we fail to realize that a great employee may do what's required of them in four hours, versus the "average Joe" who requires eight to complete the same job. We reward the one who stays late while frowning on the one who dashes out at 5 PM rushing home to their family, and in both cases, the work was completed.

> CRITICAL NOTE: As leaders, it's up to us to change the way organizations view success in today's workforce, by paving a path back to genuinely trusting those who matter most: Our Employees!

Will there be situations where someone abuses the privilege of working remotely? Of course! There will be those few who will attempt to take full advantage of a remote position, just as there are those currently who may take advantage of sick-days or cut out early when no one's looking. But in both these examples, the issue is not some flaw in the system or the working environment; it's a matter of character. A bad employee will be a lousy employee, regardless of the situation. Working remotely may just expose that character flaw much sooner.

Lastly, having remote options in place may just be the difference in business survival in the future. It seems every year organizations have to deal with severe winter storms, hurricanes, wild-fires, and other catastrophes. As mentioned earlier in the book, at the time of writing, the impact of Covid19 has been devastating to many organizations around the world. However, in the midst of this crisis, it was apparent that those organizations that could work remotely, in a time where most were going out of business, were able to survive, and some actually thrived in that environment. Because to them, it was "business as usual."

The Leadership Arena

As leaders, it is our responsibility to do everything in our power to assist our employers in achieving their organizational goals. This includes advocating for a working environment where employee trust is the catalyst for growth, and Managementship is a staple of success.

LEADERSHIP LESSONS:

1. As leaders, we must perfect the skills required to be a great manager. That specific skillset required to be a great boss, and the sixth vital compartment in your leadership vessel, is called Managementship.
2. Being transparent simply means having open and honest communication between managers and employees. When we are honest about what's going on within the organization, it builds trust, and trust builds loyalty.
3. Have Direction - If you don't take the time to study the waters you will be sailing, you may soon find yourself adrift, your direction dictated by your circumstances.
4. Plot Your Course - If you are not sure which path to take, or you keep changing direction because the seas get a little rough, your people won't follow.
5. "The most successful entrepreneurs learn, study, and reach out to mentors to improve their leadership skills."
6. The most successful leaders you will ever meet are in large part, risk takers. To them, taking calculated risks are just a part of life and a necessary ingredient on the road to greater success.

7. "If you're not making any mistakes, you're not making enough decisions."
8. You can't nurture creativity and make great decisions that grow your organization, if you are too afraid of making mistakes.
9. A great leader in perfect balance will delegate important tasks, while standing by, ready and willing to roll up their sleeves and jump in to assist (not take over), if and when the need arises.
10. As leaders, it's up to us to change the way organizations view individual success in today's workforce, by paving a path back to genuinely trusting those who matter most – our employees.

Chapter Ten: CHAMPIONSHIP

The Engine to Your Leadership Vessel, the Fuel to Your Success!

He was born on February 17th, 1963, in Brooklyn, NY, into the arms of the tough, blue-collar working parents, James and Deloris. Soon after, while he was still a little boy, his family moved to Wilmington, NC, where he would spend the rest of his growing years. Driven by his love for sports, particularly basketball, he decided to try out for his high school basketball team. Unfortunately, he was told he wasn't good enough and was rejected as a member of the team. This kind of news would generally smash the confidence of a lesser person, but not this young man. Determined to make the team in the future, he practiced day after day for an entire year, on a homemade basketball court in his backyard, built for him by his father. He not only made the team the very next year, but Michael Jordan would also go on to become one of the best MBA players of all time, grabbing a few extra local championships and a couple of Olympic Gold Medals along the way.

On January 29th, 1954, she was born in Kosciusko, Mississippi, to her unmarried parents Vernita and Vernon.

Soon after her birth, her parents separated, and she was sent to live with her grandmother, who would look after her until the age of six. From that point on, this little girl would be bounced back and forth between the safe atmosphere of her father, and the unstable, even dangerous environment with her mother. From age nine stretching into her teens, she would be sexually abused by her mother's male friends and other trusted family members while her mother was out working different jobs.

Many years later, she was finally sent back to live with her father. However, through his sometimes overly strict nurturing, this young girl transformed into a brilliant high school student and competent young woman, despite a past that would have destroyed most people. Her amazing grades and accomplishments landed her a full scholarship to Tennessee State University. Additionally, at only 19 years of age, she was offered a job where she would become the first African American woman in the state to co-host the evening news. Still determined to do more, after graduation, she went on to fill other successful TV positions in Baltimore, MD. Then, in 1983, she was asked to move to Chicago to host a morning talk show that would later be named, "The Oprah Winfrey Show." You know the rest of the story.

It's obvious; these two examples demonstrate that regardless of your circumstances, you can achieve great things. With a positive attitude, the heart of a champion, and unbending determination, you can literally achieve anything you desire. But in both amazing examples, there is a major contributor; most don't realize at first glance. More than their hard-working principles and the belief in their own abilities is the fact that they are both leaders. Without leadership, Oprah would have never been able to motivate those around her, forming and growing her own production company and building the empire we all know today. Michael would not have been able to lead his team to six NBA Championships, and go on to create the Air Jordan corporate brand with Nike, as well as many other business ventures, making him the first billionaire athlete.

In this chapter and the final phase in the building of your leadership vessel, we will discuss the elements of Championship. More than just a skill or some process to follow, Championship is the engine onboard your leadership vessel and the fuel for your success. It's the energy that keeps you driving forward, and the proverbial heart of a champion. Without this "engine" installed and running correctly, your leadership vessel will have a hard time getting underway, if it can even set sail. Let's discuss the moving parts of this critical engine called Championship!

Choose the Right Lenses

"Love and fear represent two different lenses through which to view the world. Whichever I choose, will determine what I see and think." - Marianne Williamson

Richard Spector

When we rise each morning to start our day, we have a choice. As soon as our feet hit the floor, we decide which pair of glasses we are going to put on. Which lenses are you going to look through today? Will it be the stress lenses, because we are worried about completing a critical project on-time? Or perhaps we will wear the anger lenses because we are still pissed off about having to work on a Saturday, a day initially planned to spend with friends or family. When you wake up tomorrow, which will you choose?

How we are feeling at any given moment in time, has a significant impact on our perception of the world around us. For example, if you are upset, frustrated, or just thinking negatively while driving to work, you will tend to seek out and dwell on the negative things around you. The motorcyclist that's driving too fast, or the car that's driving too slowly, or that damn morning sunlight that's blinding you, forcing you to have to pull down the visor so you can see! Even worse, these little things get us even more upset because of the lenses we are wearing. This negative attitude causes you to continue on a downward spiral throughout the day, infecting others around you as well. These examples are what leads to having one of those "bad days." We have all been there, and it's not a pretty picture.

Proof that these proverbial lenses are real, I want you to think for a moment about the types of vehicles you see on the road every day. From large to small, from sporty to luxurious, from gas-driven to fully electric, the variety is plentiful. A couple of years ago, I went shopping for a new car, and the salesman showed me a brand-new Kia Cadenza, a vehicle I was not familiar with. It was one of Kia's "upper-tier luxury models," he said, and I hadn't seen any on the road very much, if at all. I liked being unique, so I bought it! Happy, excited, and a little proud, as we all are when we first drive a new car off the lot, I headed home. What's funny is, within that 20-minute drive home, I saw the Kia Cadenza five times! It felt like everywhere I looked, I saw someone else driving the same vehicle, sometimes the exact color and everything!

Have you ever noticed that once you own a particular make and model, all of a sudden, you see them everywhere? This new awareness is because of the lenses you are looking through, and they affect how, even what you see around you. The fact is that specific type of vehicle has always been there; you just never noticed it before. Things you notice and don't notice; how you react or don't react to certain situations, are all influenced by the lenses you look through. In summary, your feelings or attitude towards life, in general, will dictate the world you experience, and ultimately your success as a leader. Furthermore, your feelings are contagious, through the vibrations you emit, so as a leader, you must be aware of and in control of the emotions you are emitting.

But here is the good news in all of this: You have a choice. You have the power to put on whichever lenses you wish when you start your day. You can choose to put on a different pair of glasses if something during your day starts to bring you down. For example, if I'm going about my day, and suddenly I find myself getting frustrated or angry at some event or situation, I simply step back, close my eyes, and take a deep breath. I imagine myself taking off my angry glasses and replacing them with a pair of happy or positive lenses. As silly as this sounds, it works because you are making a conscious effort to tell your subconscious mind to snap out of it!

It can mean the difference between honking your horn at a driver for trying to squeeze into your lane (shouting colorful metaphors they will never hear), versus gently touching your breaks to give them room, waving them in with a smile. It can mean the difference between your team losing confidence in their abilities because they sensed your doubt, versus everyone rallying together because they shared your enthusiasm!

It can make all the difference in completing that critical project ahead of schedule or winning the big game. This brings me to my next point on why having a winning attitude is so important.

> CRITICAL NOTE: Your attitude and emotions significantly impact your effectiveness as a leader.

Having a Winning Attitude.

The Leadership Arena

"I think whether you're having setbacks or not, the role of a leader is to always display a winning attitude." – Colin Powell

If you're not familiar, Colin Powell is a retired U. S. Army 4-Star General who throughout his military career, served as National Security Advisor, Commander of the US Army Forces Command, Chairman of the Joint Chiefs of Staff, as well as Secretary of State among other vital leadership positions. It's important to note here that even at that level of leadership, having a winning attitude is critical to your success, as well as the success of those around you. So regardless of your current position, whether you are in a management role or not, Championship means always displaying a winning attitude.

As I had promised at the beginning of this book, I don't want just to give you theories or opinions on different aspects of leadership, I want to help you understand the very essence of leadership, so it's more easily absorbed and retained, making it easier to pass on these lessons to those in your charge. With that, let's discuss the 7-steps to create a winning attitude, and engage that mighty ship's engine called Championship.

1. <u>Be Grateful:</u> It's called having an Attitude of Gratitude and being thankful for everything you currently have. This mindset has been proven to be beneficial in so many areas of our lives, including to develop a winning attitude. Even if your current

situation is less than desirable, you can't make things better without first being grateful for what you do have. For example, if money is tight, and you find yourself living paycheck to paycheck, struggling to make the bills, there are always things you can be grateful for. While it would be nice to have new clothes, be thankful for the clothes you do have. While a new car would be great, be grateful for the one you have that starts every morning to get you to work. Be thankful for electricity, your health, your family, and the roof over your head, even if that roof is your parent's basement. We will talk in more detail about this in my next book, but here's <u>why</u> having an 'attitude of gratitude' is so powerful. When we express how grateful we are for the things we currently have, the universe responds by providing us with more stuff for you to be thankful for.

2. <u>Associate with Winners</u>: In my last book, I spoke about the concept of changing your associations, and that same concept applies here in developing a winning attitude. We learned that if we want to elevate our life and career, then we need to change the people whom we associate with the most. For example, if one wants to become a successful senior executive, then they need to hang out with other successful senior executives. Similarly, we have already learned that feelings and emotions are contagious, so what better way to

absorb a winning attitude than by surrounding ourselves with winners? From the teachings of one of the best speakers and mentors of all time: "You will become the average of the five people you mostly associate with." – Jim Rohn

3. <u>Never Give Up</u>: While the phrase "never give up" seems a little cliché, let me give you an example of just how important it is. Let's take the game of football, for example. I'm sure we have all watched a game where one team comes out really strong, and scores let's say 21 points in the first quarter. From that point on, though both sides are statistically evenly matched, they continue to dominate the game, literally crushing the other team who ends up scoring very few points, if any. This domination is a perfect example of a group becoming demotivated and losing confidence in their ability to win. In short, they gave up. Now take, for example, the exact opposite situation. A team that is down by 21 points at the start of the fourth quarter comes back not only to even up the score but win the game! It's because they never gave up. Until the bell rings, until the whistle blows, until the fat lady sings, it's not over until it's over. These are all different phrases pointing towards the same element of Championship: Never Give Up.

4. <u>Use Affirmations</u>: Having a winning attitude means believing in yourself. Something we will discuss in detail in my next book is that a positive self-image is critical for when things get tough, but it's easier said than done. It's true, we are our own worst critic, beating ourselves up any chance we get because we genuinely want to be better. But that criticizing habitual routine, must also be countered with positive affirmations. It's the Yin and Yang of self-improvement. We need to literally remind ourselves, on a daily basis, that we are awesome! We must continuously tell our subconscious mind what we are going to accomplish as if it already happened. Be it through meditation or reading aloud words describing what you will achieve or become in the next week, month or year, affirmations are an essential ritual in developing a winning attitude. So, tell yourself every day; you are a great leader; you are a fantastic executive; you are a winner.

5. <u>Take Responsibility</u>: In an earlier chapter, we already discussed how important it is to take responsibility, and the same holds true here in this chapter on Championship. To develop a winning attitude, we must never fall into that chasm of victimhood, where we blame others for our shortcomings. Instead, take full responsibility for everything that happens to you, for it is then, and only then will you gain the power to effect real

change in your life and the lives of those around you.

6. <u>Believe</u>: Whatever goals you set for yourself, whatever dreams you have put into motion, you must believe they will come true. You may not know when, you may not even know how, but you must believe with all your heart that you will achieve the things you want.

7. <u>Team Focus</u>: The final step in creating a winning attitude is what I call Team Focus. There is no letter "I" in the word leader, thus as a leader, your ultimate focus and goal is the success of your team, not your own accolades. It's equally important to instill these values in each and every team member because once they truly understand this concept, their success is elevated to a whole new level. The quote that best describes this concept came from one of the best basketball coaches of all time. In his book titled, Eleven Rings: The Soul of Success, Phil Jackson writes: "Good teams become great ones when the members trust each other enough to surrender the ME for the WE."

Failure is Your fuel to Success!

Now that we have installed the engine onboard your leadership vessel, there is only one final ingredient remaining before we can commission your ship and set sail. This last element is by far the most significant concerning both your success as a leader and the amount of success you will experience in other areas of your life. I've placed this final topic last in the book because it's the fuel that will propel your ship forward. It's the electricity that will power the other compartments, but most importantly, it's the blood the feeds the heart of a champion. This final element and the fuel to your success is Failure.

Another example of the power of Yin and Yang is when we combine Success and Failure. Once again, one cannot exist without the other. Running from Failure, hiding from Failure, or making excuses for why we fail only hinders our ability to succeed. As mentioned previously, Failure is really an opportunity to learn and grow. When we miss a weight loss goal or fail to hit a sales target, we gain a certain amount of knowledge that can be used to increase our odds of success the next time. Lastly, Failure is part of the process of success! You can't expect to graduate college, and the very next day become a successful senior executive. You can't pick up a basketball and expect to secure an MBA contract tomorrow. You must embrace Failure and understand that as long as you learn from each situation, you are propelling yourself forward.

Before we set sail, I will end this chapter with these final words from a man who has failed more times than I dare to count:

The Leadership Arena

"The key to success is Failure. I've missed more than 9,000 shots in my career. I've lost almost 300 games. Twenty-six times, I've been trusted to take the game-winning shot and missed. I've failed over and over and over again in my life. And that is why I succeed." - Michael Jordan

LEADERSHIP LESSONS:

1. When we rise each morning to start our day, we have a choice. As soon as our feet hit the floor, we decide which pair of lenses we are going to put on.
2. Your attitude and emotions significantly impact your effectiveness as a leader.
3. "I think whether you're having setbacks or not, the role of a leader is to always display a winning attitude" – Colin Powell
4. The 7 steps to a develop a winning attitude are: Be Grateful, Associate with Winners, Never Give Up, Use Affirmations, Take Responsibility, Believe, and Team Focus.
5. Failure is your fuel to success, so don't run from it. Instead, embrace it and learn from it.

Chapter Eleven: Time to Set Sail (Epilogue)

The Commissioning of the USS Leadership

The military salute is a sign of respect dating back hundreds of years, and a custom that is still used today in all military branches. Throughout the eight weeks of Navy boot camp, the recruits are constantly saluting Company Commanders (and other officers) and calling them Sir or Ma'am, when appropriate, all designed to show respect for a person's rank and position. However, there is one exception to this common custom. When a company of naval recruits becomes sailors at recruit graduation, they perform a ceremony called "Pass and Review." This ceremony is where each company will march in formation and "pass by" their Company Commanders who are stationed (sitting) in the stands observing the graduation ceremony. It is at this point, the respective Company Commanders stand and salute the recruits for the first time, paying respect to their amazing accomplishments.

In order to keep with Naval tradition, I would, therefore, like to salute you as we bring our journey together to a close. We have covered a lot of material packed into a small book that could have easily been as long as some

The Leadership Arena

classic novel and could have just as easily overwhelmed the average reader. But here you are, standing on the pier of success looking out at the USS Leadership, a ship YOU built, now ready to set sail.

I have genuinely enjoyed our time together, and I hope you have as well. I want to encourage you to celebrate this accomplishment. Get yourself a bottle of Champaign, go out for a nice dinner, or whatever makes you feel the most joy because you deserve it. Not because you finished the book, though I do appreciate that immensely, but because of the commitment you made when you decided to read this book in the first place.

You see, I've realized from our journey together that when you decided to purchase The Leadership Arena, you were making a commitment to become a better manager, a better boss, and a better leader. That in itself sets you apart from the crowd, and for that, I sincerely thank you and salute you. Additionally, thank you again for putting your trust in me and in the Arena Trilogy series. There are so many books on the market one can choose from, and the fact that you took a chance on me, well, let me just say I am truly grateful.

By the time you read this book, I will be well underway (no pun intended) writing the third book in the series, The Abundance Arena. In this third and final installment, we will shift course a bit and dive into how to attract abundance in all areas of your life, not just your career.

Until then, I urge you to revisit these pages from time to time to remind yourself of the principles and elements needed to keep your leadership vessel sailing and on course. Additionally, it's my mission to help as many people as I can achieve the success they truly deserve, so I urge you to please share this book with anyone who you feel could benefit from its pages.

Lastly, let me leave you with some words from a song by Garth Brooks off his album "Ropin' the Wind" called The River. It was released in 1991, and its nautical theme, I believe, makes for the perfect ending to this chapter and book.

"Too many times we stand aside, and let the waters slip away; until what we put off until tomorrow, has now become today. So, don't you sit upon the shoreline and say you're satisfied; choose to chance the rapids, and dare to dance the tide."

Until we meet again: Fair Winds and Following Seas. - Richard Spector.

Bibliography

50 reasons why some businesses fail while others succeed. Retrieved from https://www.successharbor.com/why-some-businesses-fail-while-others-succeed-02132015/

Bililies Ph.D., T. (2019, January 8,). How to create an environment of lifelong learning as the leader. Retrieved from https://chiefexecutive.net/environment-lifelong-learning-leader/

Canfield, J. Live your best life from jack canfield's weekly newsletter. Retrieved from https://www.jackcanfield.com/blog/everyone-is-a-teacher/

Kenton, W. (2019a). Human resources (HR). Retrieved from https://www.investopedia.com/terms/h/humanresources.asp

Kenton, W. (2019b). Social capital. Retrieved from https://www.investopedia.com/terms/s/socialcapital.asp

Llopis, G. (2018). HR departments must urgently become human capital departments. Retrieved from https://www.forbes.com/sites/glennllopis/2018/01/0

8/hr-departments-must-urgently-become-human-capital-departments/#762598ce21a6

McRoberts, S. (2017). Here's what science says you should do to achieve greater success. Retrieved from https://www.entrepreneur.com/article/305985

Miller-Merrell, J. (2019). Benefits of workplace transparency. Retrieved from https://www.glassdoor.com/employers/blog/importance-transparent-workplace/

Nayar, V. (2013). Three differences between managers and leaders. Retrieved from https://hbr.org/2013/08/tests-of-a-leadership-transiti

Patel, S. (2015). The 12 characteristics of successful entrepreneurs. Retrieved from https://www.entrepreneur.com/article/250564

Patterson, A. M., & Hewes, R. P. (2011). Alignment is essential to effective performance, profitability. Retrieved from https://www.shrm.org/resourcesandtools/hr-topics/organizational-and-employee-development/pages/alignmentimpactonperformanceprofit.aspx

Vitaud, L. (2016). The rise and fall of HR as a department. Retrieved from https://medium.com/willbe-group/the-rise-and-fall-of-hr-as-a-department-8a8fd5ffd06a